I0062831

Praise for

STORYFIND

"A must-read for those seeking to touch hearts, stir minds, and change lives."

CHRIS DAVENPORT, Founder of Nonprofit Storytelling Conference

"Kristin and the StoryFind Films team create authentic video stories that help organizations connect with people who want to learn more about their mission. Kristin's book is a must-read for any nonprofit looking to elevate their storytelling through video."

KATHLEEN KENNEY DEVITO, Director of Marketing and Community Engagement at Homes For Our Troops

"Kristin brilliantly breaks down the art of storytelling, providing clear guidance for all nonprofits to tell stories that get results."

ANAT GERSTEIN, Founder of Anat Gerstein, Inc.: Communications that move people to action

"Full of wisdom, practical advice, and storytelling. A must-read for every nonprofit."

SCOTT HARRISON, Founder and CEO of charity: water and *New York Times* bestselling author of *Thirst*

"*StoryFind* is your nonprofit's road map to sharing transformative stories. Kristin's expert guidance will show you how to find them and tell them, and how to take great care of each of your storytellers."

VERA LEUNG, Senior Director of Content and Creative at International Rescue Committee and award-winning creative director

"Warning: Reading this book may cause your organization to no longer be the 'best kept secret.' *StoryFind* is amazing. Not only does it show you how to find the right stories in your organization; it shows you how to capture them equitably. Get a copy for every staff member. And get a copy for each of your board members."

MARC A. PITMAN, CEO of Concord Leadership Group and author of *The Surprising Gift of Doubt*

"*StoryFind* does a masterful job of making it *easy* to find and tell your organization's most impactful stories—and Kristin does it in an enjoyable and engaging way. You'll have ideas and be excited about them before you're even done with the first chapter! If you've ever thought your story-finding and storytelling could be improved, read this book immediately."

STEVEN SCREEN, Cofounder of The Better Fundraising Co.

"*StoryFind* expertly shares a systematic process for finding story nuggets and polishing them into brilliant gems with empathy, compassion, and dignity. Stories that leave the contributor whole, complete, and empowered—and call the listener to swift action!"

TAMMY ZONKER, Founder and President of Fundraising Transformed, keynote speaker, and host of *The Intentional Fundraiser Podcast*

STORYFIND

STORYFIND

The Handbook for Finding
and Telling Your Nonprofit's
Most Impactful Stories

KRISTIN SUKRAW

Copyright © 2023 by Kristin Sukraw

All rights reserved. No part of this book may be reproduced,
stored in a retrieval system or transmitted, in any form
or by any means, without the prior written consent of the
publisher, except in the case of brief quotations,
embodied in reviews and articles.

Some names and identifying details have been
changed to protect the privacy of individuals.

Cataloguing in publication information is
available from Library and Archives Canada.
ISBN 978-1-77458-415-6 (paperback)
ISBN 978-1-77458-416-3 (ebook)

Page Two
pagetwo.com

Edited by Emily Schultz
Copyedited by Crissy Calhoun
Cover and interior design by Jennifer Lum

storyfind.com

For my StoryFind team

"No one can whistle a symphony.
It takes a whole orchestra to play it."

H.E. LUCCOCK

CONTENTS

FOREWORD

STORYTELLERS hold a unique power.

From a young age, I learned this truth from people around me—my funny uncle at family gatherings, magnetic leaders in the news, and passionate figures who could draw crowds by the thousands. The common thread? Their ability to find and share stories that deeply connect with their audiences.

Take, for instance, Martin Luther King Jr. He wasn't just a civil rights leader; he was a master storyteller. His "I Have a Dream" speech was more than a call for equality; it was the story of a future he envisioned. His story inspired a nation to strive for change. That's the power of storytelling. It can drive action, ignite passion, and even change the world, one story at a time.

Storytelling, much like music, has a profound impact on our emotions. A joyful melody can lift our spirits, while a sad tune can stir deep feelings. Notice how all music, no matter how different, is made from the same notes.

Similarly, no matter how diverse, all stories are made from the same words. And just as musicians arrange notes to stir emotions, storytellers arrange words to evoke feelings, create empathy, and inspire audiences to act.

Drawing from my experiences in the film industry, I've crafted stories that transcended borders, touching hearts globally. There's a special kind of magic that happens when you find just the right story, one that connects with people's hearts. It's like hearing a song where every note just feels perfect. This magic—finding and telling the perfect story—is what Kristin's *StoryFind* is all about.

Kristin and I first met at the Nonprofit Storytelling Conference, and our shared passion for storytelling led to a close friendship. This book embodies her unique method of finding and telling stories—a method I've seen touch many lives, including mine.

StoryFind is not only a guide; it's an adventure with Sarah, its main character. As you follow her journey to uncover and shape her story, you'll find echoes of your own struggles and triumphs. Sarah's obstacles mirror the very challenges you may have faced in finding and telling stories. This connection with Sarah will help reshape your understanding of storytelling and offer a personal touch that's rare in instructional guides.

One thing I've learned is that good stories aren't only about something—they're *for* someone. They're meant to reach out and touch people, to resonate with them. *Story-Find* gives you the tools to do just that.

Kristin's Master Plan is one such tool. It's like a map, guiding you to uncover and share your best stories. This plan won't just benefit your organization; it will change you too. By finding your voice, you'll grow in confidence and in your ability to connect with those around you.

At our core, what makes us truly human is how we share and connect through stories. *StoryFind* will help you dig deep and discover the stories that draw people closer to your nonprofit's mission. With each page you turn, you start a new adventure of understanding. I'm excited for you to see where this journey takes you.

Chris Davenport
Founder, Nonprofit Storytelling Conference

CHAPTER 1

INTRODUCTION TO STORYFIND

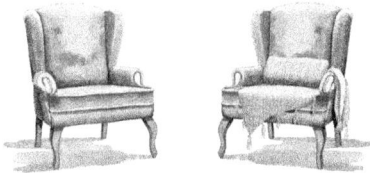

What would it mean to you if
you had a Master Plan for each story
you told? If you knew exactly how
to find your best stories?

W E ALL KNOW the power of storytelling. We know stories heal, unite, inspire, and create change and lasting impact. Stories are the backbone of your organization. But how do you find and tell stories that leave your audience with no choice but to act?

Enter StoryFind—the first ever handbook for finding and telling your best stories. I am so honored to share the simple process our clients at StoryFind Films have found successful time and time again. Our work has been featured on *The View*, on *Good Morning America*, and through highly successful national PSAs that have helped raise millions of dollars. From small local shops to large international nonprofits, and everyone in between, the process is the same. So welcome, one and all.

I'm Kristin and I will be your mentor through the StoryFind Process. Born and raised in the Midwest, I have always loved reading and dreaming. In my adult life, I found my way into the world of storytelling through a back door. I began my career as a mental health therapist, working primarily with teenagers. While I loved my clients, I was very intrigued by the work my husband was doing with his film production company. He had assembled an amazing team of empathetic filmmakers who were telling the stories of nonprofits to help them raise more money.

I wanted to be a part of it—there's nothing quite like being on set on production day!—so I wiggled my way in over the course of a year, volunteering to work on more and more projects. There was not much difference between sitting in the chair as a therapist and as an interviewer with a nonprofit storyteller. I began to experiment with counseling techniques to help storytellers feel safe and understood. We worked to create on-set environments where all the film gear would seem to fade into the background for the storyteller.

One of my fondest memories from those early years with StoryFind Films is the time I got to spend with a woman named Desirae who had attended a small HBCU in Selma, Alabama. We were hired by the university's development department to tell the stories of former students who had gone on to find success. We had everything set up for Desirae's interview in a beautiful historic building, waited and waited, and she didn't show up. The school's development director called her, and she admitted she had cold feet. So, we talked with Desirae, and she said she would be willing to try again the next day.

In part because of my counseling background, our film sets are a place of honor and respect, which means giving our storytellers what they need to feel safe. In this case, what Desirae needed was time to process and explore various aspects of her life and how they had impacted her future. We knew this up front, so the crew settled in to hear her story and didn't rush her. We sat together for about two hours (for a two-minute final video) as she explored her life's journey through laughter and tears. At the end of her interview, she stood up and embraced me with one of my favorite hugs of all time and said, "You don't know what you've done for me." The opportunity to share her story on behalf of the university meant the world to her. It meant that her journey had not been for nothing; she was able to inspire donors to give so that others who struggle like she had would have the chance to change their lives through education.

Storytelling changes people. Giving people the chance to tell their stories means you are giving their journey meaning and purpose. My passion is helping people make sense of what they have experienced by giving them a platform to share their stories, and you can do this too!

For the very first time, there is a resource that teaches you how to find and tell your best stories in a way that honors your storytellers and helps you achieve your goals. I am so excited to present to you *StoryFind*. I promise to teach you all that I have learned along the way in a highly applicable format. You will learn the full, five-step Story-Find Process:

- Create a Master Plan
- Find and Select Your Best Stories
- Organize Your Stories
- Interview with Skill
- Edit for Maximum Impact

Though I own a film production company, this book assumes that you are telling stories in various mediums. It focuses mainly on how to tell longer-form stories in video, audio, or print, but each of these longer-form stories can be edited down to a variety of lengths to maximize audience engagement.

While *StoryFind* is applicable to any organization that is telling its stories, this book is geared toward nonprofits and your desire to tell stories to drive donor engagement or action. Therefore, all the examples shared, and the story I tell at the beginning of each chapter, are specific to nonprofits. If you are not part of a nonprofit, please know that everything will still help you connect with your audience! I am glad you are here too.

Before we dive into the process, I want to set the stage a little bit. Why tell stories? Because excellent storytelling:

- Creates human connection
- Breaks through the noise in your audience's world
- Clearly and succinctly communicates who you are
- Simplifies what could be a complex organizational strategy
- Allows you to be personal
- Attracts new donors
- Expands relationships with existing supporters
- Creates easily shareable content
- Gives your organization the voices of those who have actually experienced change

Do you see your organization's goals reflected in this list? What would it mean to you if you had a Master Plan for each story you told? If you knew exactly how to find your best stories? If after you selected a story, you knew how to organize it for maximum impact? What if you could draw a storyteller out in a way that made them feel both safe and empowered? And finally, what if you had a strategy to edit down your stories in a way that would connect deeply with your audience's hearts?

I am here to simplify your life and help you make the most of your most valuable assets—your stories! Whether you are looking to raise more money, recruit volunteers, or retain and challenge existing supporters, *StoryFind* will help you reach your goals.

At the beginning of each chapter, you will read the story of Sarah, who works at a fictional nonprofit called KidsKan (not related to any organization that might exist with a similar name). Sarah's story gives you a real-world application of the principles you are about to learn. While Sarah's story is fictional, she is an amalgamation of several of our clients who have walked successfully through the StoryFind Process.

I am so glad you are here and look forward to building a relationship with you. Let me introduce you to the KidsKan story, and we will get started!

Introduction to the KidsKan Story

Sarah walked into her office at KidsKan, a regional non-profit organization whose mission is to build confidence in kids and help break the cycle of poverty through direct services and advocacy. She felt nervous but incredibly excited. She had spent the last two years feeling discouraged and frustrated in her role at KidsKan, but it seemed as if things were about to change.

The KidsKan mission was one she felt called to since high school. She used to serve as a table leader for their after-school program and fell in love with the kids she met. She went off to college and returned home with a degree in marketing and a minor in family studies. In the four years she had been gone, KidsKan had grown significantly from operating at one location in the inner city to also providing services in two nearby towns.

KidsKan needed help supporting this growth, and Sarah felt she was up to the task. A role was created for her that served the needs of both the marketing and development departments. It wasn't long before she felt overworked. On top of trying to do the work of two (or three!) people, she wasn't able to do the number one thing she knew could drive results. Every time she suggested telling their stories, her executive director, Maria, said a definitive no. The most common objections Sarah heard were that the kids they served were minors, and KidsKan didn't want to make anyone feel ashamed, victimized, or exploited.

Sarah understood these reasons and would never intentionally do anything to hurt the kids she loved so much. But she also knew how genuinely proud of their growth a lot of the kids were. She regularly heard from staff that program graduates came back to say thank you. And on top of that, family members of current students came in to report all of the positive growth in their children. Many of them would do anything they could to help ensure KidsKan would be around to give other kids the same opportunities their families received.

So much of Sarah's role depended on her ability to share the successes of her favorite kids and families. Without being able to share their stories, she felt disillusioned and ineffective. If truth be told, Sarah had started inquiring about positions elsewhere.

Today, though, change was in the air! Maria had just returned from a national conference on storytelling for nonprofit organizations. Enticed by a friend with the idea of a week at a beachfront property with like-minded professionals, Maria (herself near burnout) went with very little expectation that the concept of storytelling would apply to KidsKan. While she was there, however, she attended a session by StoryFind, and her understanding of what could be was turned upside down.

Today was Maria's first day back in the office, and she immediately sat down with Sarah to teach her everything she'd learned.

Maria's words were the last thing Sarah was expecting to hear: "Sarah, I was wrong. I have spent years depriving these kids and families of the opportunity to share their stories. I thought I was protecting them by not asking them to share, but I see now that maybe I was communicating to them that their growth was something to be ashamed of."

Sarah sat quietly, taking it all in and wondering what Maria would say next.

"Sarah, what would you say if I told you that you have my full support to start sharing our stories?"

"I would say, 'I'll get started today!'" Sarah broke into a grin.

"Would you know where to begin?" asked Maria.

Sarah hesitated. "I guess I'm not entirely sure. I mean, I have heard a lot of amazing stories over the years. I guess I would have to really sit down and think about it."

"At this conference," said Maria, "I learned about the StoryFind Process. It's like nothing I've ever heard before. They've put together a step-by-step approach that we can follow to find and tell our best stories. Their approach also ties in what drives an audience to act. So it's more than just storytelling. It's storytelling that moves people to get involved. I think it could be exactly what we need."

Maria described StoryFind's five-step method for finding and telling your best stories:

- Create a Master Plan
- Find and Select Your Best Stories
- Organize Your Stories
- Interview with Skill
- Edit for Maximum Impact

"That sounds good, but a little overwhelming!" Sarah said.

"I think it might be in the beginning, but over time, if it goes well, I really see storytelling becoming the bulk of your job," Maria replied. "Take this binder on the StoryFind Process. You can find their resources online, too, but this is something they gave us at the conference, and it contains all of my notes from their session as well. I would encourage you to start at the beginning and walk through the process in its entirety for the first story you tell."

Sarah took the binder and walked back to her office. She couldn't help but think, "Is this really happening?" She knew she was about to fall in love with KidsKan all over again, and she was going to get started today.

Conclusion

Again, I welcome you into my world and process of storytelling. We'll hear more from Sarah and her KidsKan story at the start of each chapter, followed by a how-to section where I take you step by step through executing the StoryFind Process.

Before we close our introduction, I want to recap what we learned in this chapter:

- Your organization can benefit greatly by collecting and sharing stories

- Individuals, both those telling their own stories and those collecting them, grow through this process and feel rewarded

- There is a system you can use to tell your stories simply and effectively

I am thrilled that you are on this journey with me. Are you ready to get started? Let's dive in together!

CHAPTER 2

THE MASTER PLAN

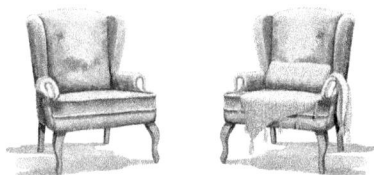

Every successful story
starts with a plan.

'M KIND OF AN organization nerd. Let's take my closet, for instance. I find so much satisfaction in knowing that everything has a home. Everything is systematically sorted and matched, creating something that (to me) looks beautiful. Yes, it's color coordinated, and no, it isn't overflowing.

I believe deeply in the value of sifting through what doesn't have a place, so that what *does* have a place can be clearly seen and given a spotlight. Purposeful storytelling and closet organization are one and the same. Both require a system that ultimately highlights what you want the world to see and that helps you get rid of anything that may be a distraction.

Where do you start when it comes to story creation? The first step in the StoryFind Process is creating a Master Plan, and I promise it is a lot more fun than it sounds. Your Master Plan will become your treasure map, your compass, your guiding star leading you forward in your storytelling quest. You'll know and understand your goals, target audience, and logistics of how your story will be used.

I actually can't wait to walk through this process with you because I know you'll feel proud of yourself in the end. In this chapter, we begin with the KidsKan story—you'll see Sarah craft her Master Plan in real time—and then you'll learn how to create your own Master Plan that leads you to storytelling success.

The KidsKan Story: The Master Plan

"How can I capture one of our stories by the end of the day?" Sarah asked herself. Everything in her wanted to call up one of her old students and ask them to come tell their story that afternoon.

Sarah was always known for putting the cart before the horse, and thankfully before she could touch her phone, her toughest marketing teacher's voice echoed through her memory. "Slow down, Sarah! What would they be telling their story for? Who would see it? Would you be highlighting a specific program? Is this story going to be a video? In print?"

Sarah smiled at the memory of someone reining in her full-steam-ahead approach to life, but then her emotional brain fought back a bit. "Something is better than nothing, though, right?" She was discouraged before she even started. "What should this process look like?" she asked herself.

Slowing down to learn was something that Sarah felt stood in her way; however, she really wanted to get this right. There was a lot at stake with Maria actually trusting her to tell a story for the first time. She glanced down at the material Maria had handed her an hour earlier.

Opening the binder, she flipped to the first section and saw the words *Master Plan* written boldly in front of her.

The Master Plan was organized into two headings: Messaging Strategy and Logistics. Under the Messaging Strategy heading were the following categories:

- Objective
- Define Success
- Target Audience
- One Big Idea

Under the Logistics heading, Sarah read:

- Story Medium
- Target Length
- Call to Action
- Placement

Excitement struck again as Sarah decided that her goal for the end of the day was to fill out this Master Plan. Stepping back would give her storytelling an anchor and a purpose. Her marketing professor would be proud, she told herself.

Worksheets were a favorite part of Sarah's school years, so she had high hopes for this one. She decided to take it top to bottom and give each section the attention it deserved.

"What is my objective for telling a story?" she asked herself. Her gut response was "to raise money, of course!" But she knew there was more to it than that.

The community had lost touch with the heart of Kids-Kan. As the organization had grown, their donor base had actually shrunk. KidsKan received government funding and had successfully applied for and received a handful of multiyear grants. Their major donors had stayed intact through the years, but because of Sarah's lack of ability to tell success stories, their general donor base was uncertain as to what KidsKan's needs were and how to support them.

"Aha! So, communicating our needs will help us raise more money!" Sarah said out loud as she quickly jotted down "communicating our needs" in the box marked Objective.

And there were certainly a lot of needs. Amongst other things, KidsKan offered parenting coaching and training programs. They ran after-school programs for children whose parents worked late. Their stable-housing program worked to create a network of both temporary and permanent homes for families facing housing inse-curity. And then there were the annual initiatives like the Thanksgiving dinner boxes, a Christmas store, and a summer day camp.

It was a lot. She thought back to where it all began: the after-school program—now named KidsKorner. Maybe the best place to start was reminding donors of KidsKan's roots as an organization. It would be something familiar to the donors and not too overwhelming for Sarah. Reintro-ducing the program and sharing its success seemed like a good place to start; however, Sarah knew that she needed to share not only the successes but the program's needs. The KidsKorner program relied solely on private donors to fund it, and she wondered if there was anything specific the program was lacking. Coming up empty, she decided to walk down the hall and talk to the after-school program director, Bryant.

Bryant's office was overflowing as usual, and Sarah smiled as she looked around at what looked like a teenage boy's bedroom or a gym coach's office. Bryant was just walking in himself and welcomed Sarah to grab a seat.

Tossing a bag of soccer balls on the floor, Sarah sat down in a chair and got right down to business. "What do you need, Bryant? If we were asking our donors to help raise funds for your program, where would you start?"

Bryant smiled, reached into his desk drawer, and pulled out a list. He handed it over to Sarah and gave her a moment to read through it. There were six items on his wish list: some large and some small, some were physical items, and some required a fair bit of human resources:

- Playgrounds built at our two new campuses
- New mentors
- Fresh paint at our original campus
- Snacks—we are always running low
- An assistant director
- Toy room restocked

"It's a lot," he said. "I sometimes feel like we are the forgotten program. I don't mean to sound like I feel sorry for us, but we don't receive the funding that the other programs do. And I feel like we are slipping behind. I want our kids to have both a safe place to come after school and also a quality place."

"What is the one thing on this list you wish would happen first?" Sarah asked.

"Recruiting mentors" was Bryant's definitive reply. "And actually the playgrounds are another immediate need. I want people to understand that when the kids are here at the after-school program, it's often the only time they get to be kids. They've been in classrooms all day and there is so much pent-up energy. We try to be creative with outdoor activities, but playgrounds help the children to be much more self-directed. They allow for creativity and physical activity without the input of an adult. I know we need mentors, but playgrounds are a close second on my list."

Sarah thanked Bryant for his time. She found her mind wandering as she slowly made her way back to her office. "This could be cool," she said to herself. "We do need to do a push for mentors, but I think building the two playgrounds may be a perfect secondary goal. That way if people don't feel like they can give their time, maybe they will give their money."

Sarah walked over to her worksheet and filled in the square labeled Objective: "To recruit mentors for our after-school program and build two new playgrounds."

Whew! Okay, this was starting to feel good. A plan was beginning to take shape. The next words on the worksheet were *Define Success*. StoryFind's document urged her to quantify the success if possible.

Sarah knew from Bryant that success to him meant that every kid in the program would be matched with a mentor they would meet with once a week. There was a deficit of about thirty mentors across their three campuses. They also needed a waiting list of people to call when new kids entered the program. With that in mind, Sarah wrote "recruiting forty new mentors."

She did not know how much two new playgrounds would cost, so she hit a roadblock. At the same time, her phone chimed with a reminder that a meeting was starting in ten minutes. Sarah felt a little disappointed because she wanted to reach her goal of finishing by the end of the day, but she was beginning to understand the value of the Master Plan and knew she needed to give it proper attention. Before her meeting, she stopped in Maria's office and asked if she could meet with her the next morning to see if she was on track. They were both so excited, they decided to meet first thing!

The next morning, Sarah and Maria sat in comfortable chairs in the coffee shop next door to KidsKan. It was important to Sarah that she slowed herself down as much as possible, encouraging her brain to think outside her gut reactions, so she had chosen a place that removed day-to-day distractions and ignited creativity. Sarah had so much adrenaline that she decided to skip the caffeine and dive right into what she had created so far.

"I decided to talk to Bryant and focus our first story on KidsKorner's needs," she began. "I think it will be the best way to draw back our supporters' attention and attract new donors. They are already familiar with the program and have demonstrated that they want to give to this kind of work."

Maria smiled.

"So, this is what I have written for our Objective," Sarah read. "To recruit mentors for our after-school program and build two new playgrounds." She paused to see what Maria's response would be.

Maria was thoughtful. "I certainly understand your logic, Sarah. I'm guessing you're thinking some people can give time and others give monetarily, right?"

Sarah nodded.

"One of the things that StoryFind taught us is to be specific. A challenge you will run into as you start looking for stories is someone who can emotionally articulate the need for both mentors and a new playground," Maria said.

She went on: "When you go after more than one goal, you're likely to get less of a response. An audience left with a choice may take their time to think about that choice. And when action isn't immediate, it might not ever happen. What if we started with one of these initiatives and then did another story to support the other?"

That made sense to Sarah, but how was she supposed to choose? "There is a great need for both of these things," Sarah reflected to Maria.

"Yes, you're right. I do have a thought, though. This will be our first story we share with our audience, and we want as many people to respond as possible. The number of people who can be involved in building two new playgrounds is much higher than the number of people who will respond to being mentors. So, what if we start with that?" Maria suggested gently.

"I think that sounds perfect!" Sarah responded. "One of the underlying goals of this project for me is reengaging our stagnant donor base. Giving to playgrounds is an opportunity to reengage everyone and not just those few who have the time to serve as mentors."

"You've done great work so far, and I can't wait to see what comes next. When we get to the office, I'll grab you the quote from our contractor to build those playgrounds, so you'll have specific goal numbers. They included it in their initial scope of work, but we didn't have funds to complete them." Maria and Sarah walked back to the office together in the warmth of the late summer air.

With the quote from the contractor in hand, Sarah sat down at her desk and changed her Master Plan document to read:

Objective: To raise funds to build two new playgrounds

Define Success: Raising $150k

Sarah decided to keep moving with the process. Next up was defining the Target Audience. This was going to be a little easier. Sarah had studied how to create personas in school, and in her first year on the job, she had worked up three KidsKan donor profiles she named Community Building Craig, Safe Place Sandy, and Kids First Kaitlyn.

Because of this work, she knew exactly what her audiences responded to. This story was going to be broad, targeting all of the personas, though Sarah reminded herself that she would have the luxury of telling stories directly to each of her personas in the future.

For Target Audience, Sarah wrote down:

People who:

- Care deeply about systemic change in our community and believe that creating that change starts in childhood
- Are concerned about the safety and development of our community's children
- Are motivated by seeing real change and feeling like they are making a difference.

Satisfied with her outline of her Target Audience, Sarah pressed on to the final piece of the Strategy section of the Master Plan: the One Big Idea. Something clicked! This is what Maria had been talking about that morning. Adding in too much would muddy a clear path to action. She was starting to see it now. StoryFind's One Big Idea asked for something simple: a basic idea that would guide the entirety of the story.

She thought for a few minutes before writing "Our children need two new playgrounds in order to learn, build friendships, understand life skills, and release physical energy. They are key to creating healthy children." This seemed a little wordy, so she tried to simplify it. Finally, she wrote, "Playgrounds are key to creating healthy children."

Now that the strategy portion of the Master Plan was complete, Sarah moved into the Logistics phase and came up with the following:

Story Medium: Video

Target Length: Three to four minutes

Call to Action: To be determined

Placement: Fall gala, newsletter campaign, social media

It had taken her a few hours, but Sarah was satisfied. She thought back to just one day ago when she didn't know where to start. Here she was just twenty-four hours later and she had a clear road map in place for telling a story that she was confident would drive results for KidsKan.

She couldn't wait to take the next step.

Application: The Master Plan

Every successful story starts with a plan, as we've just learned from Sarah. In the StoryFind Process, the first step is to create your own Master Plan. This one document guides your every effort going forward, and as such, spending time on its creation is the *most important* thing you can do for your story.

Surprisingly, the Master Plan is also the most skipped step in our process. If you're like me (and Sarah!), you want to get to the more fun parts of storytelling: taking a story and molding it into something beautiful. Let's be honest, while I love organizing my closet, I don't love the process of planning where everything will go. However, starting with a Master Plan helps anchor those of us with creative spirits to the ultimate purpose in what we are doing. And telling a story without purpose can lead to a confused, unresponsive audience.

So, let's dive into what a Master Plan looks like. The first part of the Master Plan is called the Messaging Strategy. The creation of this part of the plan centers on your answers to four mission-critical questions:

- What is your objective for telling a story?
- How will you define success?
- Who is the target audience you are trying to reach?
- What is your One Big Idea?

The answers to these four questions guide every choice you make going forward.

The second piece of your Master Plan is Logistics. It outlines four additional critical components for launching your story well:

- Story Medium
- Target Length
- Call to Action
- Placement

I want to walk you through each piece of the Master Plan step by step because completing it in a way that drives action requires a lot of intentionality. It requires you to look at the bigger picture, ask yourself hard questions, and answer with honesty.

MASTER PLAN

MESSAGING STRATEGY

What Is Your Goal? Identify one specific goal you're trying to reach.

How Will You Define Success? How will you know if you accomplished your goal?

Who Is Your Audience? Is your audience current donors or people who have never heard of your organization before?

What Is Your Story's One Big Idea? What is the one thing you want your audience to remember?

LOGISTICS

Story Medium How will you tell your story? Video? Audio? Print?

Target Length How long do you hope your project will be?

Call to Action What do you want your audience to do with what they just experienced?

Placement Where will your story live? Live event? Newsletter? Blog?

Objective

Let's start with the first piece of the Master Plan: the objective for telling your story. The why. Why do you want to tell a story? What do you hope it will accomplish? Creating your objective means getting specific. You can have a broad goal with some secondary goals, but focus on the main objective you want to accomplish with the story you're telling.

Why be specific? Well, if you know that your goal in sharing a story is to raise more funds, there are very formulaic steps that you can take to move your audience to action. If your goal is to highlight one area of your nonprofit, you will know up front to find a story from that genre of stories. If you want to create awareness about what you do, you might find a handful of success stories to weave together that encapsulate the entirety of your organization. Or perhaps you find one story that touches on the multiple facets of what you do.

When you are specific in creating your objective, you are more likely to choose a story that yields the results you want to achieve. This step also results in a more engaged audience that knows what you want them to do because of what they experienced. Just like Sarah, who needed to choose between the goals of recruiting mentors and building playgrounds, remember that a story without direction leads to a disengaged audience.

I want to make a side note here. In going through the StoryFind Process, you will likely find many good stories that don't necessarily fit the goals you are hoping to achieve.

Set them aside for later use. Do not be afraid to create well-defined goals and to honor those goals by selecting a story most likely to help your organization realize them.

The most common storytelling goals we see from organizations are: communicating needs, changing perceptions, creating awareness, celebrating a milestone or accomplishment, and encouraging giving. Let's explore what each of these looks like practically.

Communicating needs can be general or specific. For an example of a general need, we often hear from nonprofits that they think their audience has forgotten about them. This was the case with Lutheran Braille Workers (the world's largest producer of Braille and Specialized Large Print Bibles); they approached us to create a video for their seventy-fifth-anniversary celebration. The goal was two-fold: to celebrate a milestone and to remind the audience that fulfilling their mission was still incredibly important and relevant.

Of course, you can also communicate specific needs through storytelling. At StoryFind Films, we worked with a large regional service provider whose mission is to offer hope to individuals and families in the Midwest by providing early childhood education, offering housing solutions, and engaging community leaders to coach those in need.

Even writing that sentence is a mouthful! They do so much and have such a deep impact on our community. They have an overview video demonstrating the entirety of their story, but they also aren't afraid to share stories that highlight specific programs and display individual needs. In fact, we recently produced a video for them with the goal of communicating their need for coaches to work with at-risk youth seeking stable housing. The specificity of the story they chose to tell meant the audience was laser-focused on helping solve this one issue.

Changing audience perceptions is the second goal that comes up frequently, especially for organizations that have been around for a long time. Maybe things have slowly changed over the years, and you need to get an aging donor base up to speed and introduce a younger audience to the "new you."

Or perhaps you want to change perceptions about an issue you might be solving in your community. For example, with the project for the regional service provider, the misconception was that these homeless teens had access to shelter services, which you might find in a more urban area. However, in the vastly rural Midwest with no centralized shelter, homelessness actually meant young people would couch-surf from house to house or live out of vehicles with no means of attaining a permanent dwelling. Helping people understand the issue and how the organization was solving it meant clarity for their mission and a low barrier of entry for donors to jump in to help become part of the solution.

Finally, there are organizations in which one arm of what they do seems to be all their audience knows or cares about. We worked with an organization that did anti-sex-trafficking work centered on border monitoring between two countries. This arm of the organization generated a lot of support. But the rest of their work was not as well known. They also did aftercare with the intercepted girls and had children's homes for street children in larger cities. Through storytelling, we communicated the need for funding these other areas of service.

Changing audience perceptions is often best done through the voices of those you serve. They are living proof that your organization has changed, grown, or does so much more than what your audience might think.

Sometimes creating general awareness of your cause might be your only goal in telling a story. Make an ask at the end, and be bold in regularly reminding people that you exist and are important. Not every story has to be your centerpiece story. Consistently sharing simple stories creates awareness and reminds audiences that you are actually doing great work.

Next, getting more specific by celebrating your milestones or accomplishments is an incredibly effective way to connect with your audience. When Lutheran Braille Workers celebrated its seventy-fifth anniversary, they put on a gala and shared story after story of impact. They had a lot to celebrate with their supporters who made what they do possible.

Finally, every story you tell can have the goal of encouraging your audience to support your organization. But sometimes you will know from the beginning that your express purpose in sharing a story is to make an ask at the end. Knowing this is the goal up front should change the way you tell the story and build to an explicit ask (which we dive into in Chapter 8).

These are the five main objectives we see at Story-Find. Once your objective is defined, stick to it. When a good story comes along that doesn't really align with your project goals, it can be so tempting to follow it. But when there is a Master Plan in place, you can go back to it as your anchor. It will remind you of *why* you are sharing a story. Everything else (yes, even that amazing story you just found!) has to be put on the back burner in order to accomplish your primary goal.

How Will You Define Success?

How you define success can be an intimidating question, and this is the one I see organizations brush off most often. It *is* challenging to think about when it comes to storytelling, but don't you want to know if your efforts paid off?

Let's break it down together. Often, telling a story is tied up in a larger initiative like a gala or capital campaign. As a result, you might be unable to trace a measurable result to your story alone. That's okay! Still try to come up with a way to know if it is successful. Maybe it's the number of views on YouTube if your story ends up in video format. Maybe it's a dollar amount linked to the release of a specific story within the overall campaign. Don't be afraid to get creative, and please push yourself to come up with some way to know if you were successful. At the end of the day, keep asking yourself, "How will I know if my story did what I hoped it would do?"

Looking at it from another angle, perhaps your success is simply defined by whether or not you accomplished your objective. For example, do more people know about you? Did you receive more volunteer applications? Did more money come from this year's event versus events in the past? Did you acquire new donors or reengage stagnant ones? Did your current donors give more than usual? Does your website have more hits?

Simply put, after you define your goal, define how you will know when you've done what you said you were going to do. This accountability will keep you on track to tell the right stories in ways that actually connect to your target audience.

Define Your Audience

Once you've defined your goals and know how you will reach them, it's time to describe your target audience.

This is the best time to interview yourself with a lot of honesty. It's common to be so focused on your mission and those you serve that knowing your audience may not come as naturally as defining a goal for a story. However, if you understand who they are, you can understand their core motivations and desires. If you understand their motivations and desires, you can connect with them in a way that prompts action.

If knowing your audience is something you struggle with, here are some questions you can ask yourself to begin to outline a profile (or profiles) of the people you are trying to reach:

- Who are they?
- What are they like?
- What commonalities do they share?
- How are they different from each other?
- What motivates them?
- Do you know how they came to be a part of your audience?
- Did a particular story you've told in the past resonate with this group?
- What about that story seemed to motivate them to action?

Knowing your audience means you know how to motivate them, which in turn will drive results.

You can tell one story and attempt to connect to your wider audience, or you can segment your audience into personas and target each group individually. While it is great to have the resources to get specific, casting that broad net to the entirety of your audience can also be fruitful. This is what we will see Sarah do with KidsKan.

Ohio State University professor Steven Reiss conducted a study on basic human desires involving more than six thousand participants. He found that sixteen basic desires guide nearly all meaningful behavior. Think about it. No matter how many segments you divide your audience into, sixteen core human desires motivate us all!

Here is the list of desires from his study: power, independence, curiosity, acceptance, order, saving, honor, idealism, social contact, family, status, vengeance, romance, eating, physical exercise, and tranquility.

Reiss said, "These desires are what drive our everyday actions and make us who we are. What makes individuals unique is the combination and ranking of these desires."

Understanding which of these desires is most important to your audience means you have the chance to make a profound impact on both their hearts and minds.

Let's talk about audience segmentation. For our purposes, I will not dive into the how-tos of segmenting your audience because that would fill an entire book! But I do want to touch on the concept at a higher level.

Audiences can be profiled based on their demographics, psychographics, interests, and behaviors. If you are new to this concept, I'd like to present a personal example based on a student recruitment campaign I worked on for a nonprofit university. They segmented their audience personas into the following: Transfer Tara, Social Sam, First Gen Fred, Academic Amy, and Returning Roberto. The names alone are highly descriptive, but this university also developed detailed profiles of what each persona was like. We were able to use that to recruit storytellers within each of the specific personas. The result was a highly successful campaign because the targeted viewers were able to see themselves and their desires reflected in a specific storyteller.

This is something you can do as well! Begin by defining each of your audience segments. Once defined, ask yourself, What are each segment's top three motivating desires? For example, First Gen Fred is motivated to attend college because he values independence, honor, and family. He is looking for a place that feels safe and where he feels supported and knows that there are people available to talk to if he has questions.

There is so much power in speaking to the core desires of specific groups; however, if you can only tell one story that must connect with your entire audience, look to see if any desires overlap. For example, all prospective university students are striving to obtain an education and skills that will give them better opportunities in the future. You can use these common denominators to shape how you tell the story, the language you use, the storyteller you select, and the call to action you place at the end.

While telling one story really well is better than telling no stories, the bottom line is that the more specifically you can reach your audience's basic human desires, the more you can motivate them to action. If they are motivated to act, you can serve more, do more, and change the world more!

One Big Idea

Once your audience is defined, you have the opportunity to get one message across and drive them to one call to action. Crafting your One Big Idea is the fourth and final section of the Messaging Strategy section of your Master Plan.

We've all seen videos or read stories where we walk away wondering what we are supposed to do with what we just saw. This often occurs when a story becomes a pot of stew, as I like to call it. Each department throws in a little of this or a little of that. We are told we need to give a nod to this initiative or talk about all five programs, oh, and maybe we should also mention our food drive. You get the picture.

We had one client decide to abandon their Master Plan in post-production. They had five department heads all vying to be the loudest voice, and there were, I kid you not, ninety-six comments (most of them contradicting each other) during the review of our first editing draft. A pot of stew means no focus, which leaves your audience without clarity; they are uncertain about what to do with what they just experienced.

This is reality: audiences act upon what they understand, they can only digest a little at a time (even if you do a whole lot more), and you have to make sure the barrier to acting is free and clear. Do *not* try to superimpose multiple ideas into a story and expect the story to be impactful. Audiences will resist the confusion. *Do* think through your One Big Idea up front, and it will serve as an anchor to your storytelling.

Big ideas are simple. Children in India need your help now. Our group home needs to be renovated, and your gift will help restore it. Unhoused people need coats this winter, and you can help. Playgrounds are key to creating healthy children.

Find your One Big Idea and use it to guide everything else: the interview questions or script you write, the programs you choose to include or exclude, the location you choose for filming, etc. When you are revising or editing your story, keep everything that serves the One Big Idea and let go of anything that might pull an audience away from it.

Having a One Big Idea also safeguards you from well-intentioned colleagues who may want to start making that pot of stew. You can quickly point them back to the One Big Idea and put the rest of the ideas on the shelf for next time.

We've come to the end of the Messaging Strategy section of the Master Plan! Well done. You are well on your way to understanding purposeful storytelling. The second part of the Master Plan is Logistics. In this section, you will be defining your Story Medium, Target Length, Call to Action, and Placement.

Story Medium

This section asks you to define if you are going to be telling your story via video, print, or audio. Oftentimes, the answer is more than one! Don't be afraid to repurpose a gala video in a newsletter following the event, or to place a snippet of the video's audio in a radio or podcast ad. You can get creative with using one story in multiple channels. New audiences can be reached, and those who have already heard the story will likely listen again and become more attached to it.

Target Length

For video, you can choose a target length in minutes. For print, the length might be determined by word count. There is no magical length for how long a story should be, but a good rule of thumb is to make it short enough to hold your audience's attention and long enough to be effective. Stories between two and four minutes are often the most effective video length for everyday use. Similarly, a story in print should be short, sweet, and read for no longer than a minute (about 150 words).

Call to Action

Always tell your audience what to do with what they just experienced. Every story is an invitation for audience participation with your organization. Sometimes your call to action will be determined on the front end, but you may want to wait until your story is in editing to decide on the specific terminology you will use. Oftentimes a storyteller will say an amazing sentence that shapes how you word your call to action for your audience. We will see this play out as Sarah waits to determine her specific call to action for her KidsKan story.

Placement

Decide up front where you would like your story to live. Would you like to produce something for your gala? Find the face of your next social media campaign? Produce television commercials? Determining where you would like this story to live means you'll purposefully select a story that will succeed where you place it.

As you determine your Story Medium, Target Length, Call to Action, and Placement, you will be organized and armed for successful use of your final product. There have been times when organizations want us to produce a video but have no idea what they are going to do with it. My heart has grieved many amazing stories that have never seen the light of day or never received the attention they deserve. Honor your storytellers (and your own efforts!) with a plan of how the story will serve your organization.

Conclusion: The Master Plan

As you've just learned, creating a Master Plan is the first step in the StoryFind Process. Its creation will ensure you are crafting an intentional, purposeful, and impactful story that drives results for your organization. This chapter covered a lot of ground, and your answers to the Master Plan's questions will truly serve as your foundation for the entirety of your storytelling efforts. As you get started planning your next story, remember to ask:

- What are my goals?
- How will I know I reached them?
- Who is my target audience?
- What is my One Big Idea?
- What is my story's medium?

- What is its target length?
- How will I call my audience to action?
- Where will my story live?

This intentionality up front will propel your organization forward with clarity and purpose.

CHAPTER 3

THE STORY HUNT

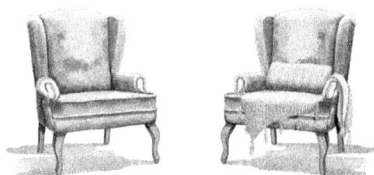

Trust and vulnerability are
the top two things to look for when
searching for a story.

T WOULD BE MY DREAM to live in a world where all I did was track down the best storytellers. I love the fun in creating an initial list of potential names. I even love the challenge of those storytellers not being readily available, and the strategy behind tracking them down. I love creating Discovery Interview questions and meeting with potential storytellers to learn what is most important to their hearts.

The pressure is off in this phase—you just get to listen! And the best part is you'll often end up with more stories than you can handle. It is so satisfying to present to clients not only a story that fits their current project's goals but also additional stories they can use in so many other ways. I think you're going to love this part too. Let's check back in with Sarah, and then we'll work together on finding your best storytellers.

The KidsKan Story: The Story Hunt

With her Master Plan road map in place, Sarah opened her binder to the next section of the StoryFind Process. In bold letters, she saw *The Story Hunt* written on the page in front of her. Intrigued, she began to read. Step one instructed her to start with a list of names of potential storytellers. Step two involved conducting Discovery Interviews. And step three outlined parameters for selecting a storyteller.

This was exciting, but Sarah felt a little intimidated. She decided it would be best to take one step at time. She knew she needed to figure out how to communicate the need for a new playground, but she wasn't sure a storyteller could adequately articulate how a playground impacted their life. Her mind started to spiral with the thought that she may not be able to achieve her goals. She coached herself not to dwell on the outcome just yet and instead to trust the process that was laid out in front of her.

She took a deep breath and said to herself, "So, step one: start with a list of three to five potential storytellers." StoryFind outlined a list of criteria of what to look for— people who:

- Trust you
- Demonstrate vulnerability
- Can display emotion
- Make you think, "I bet there's more to this story"
- You like interpersonally

Sarah was about six years out from having worked directly with any of the kids herself, but she immediately thought of two names: Celeste and Stephen. Both were in college and planned to return to the community to serve in meaningful ways. She jotted down their names. She knew she needed input from staff who were more recently connected to potential storytellers. She headed off down the hall to speak with Bryant again.

"Knock, knock! Me again!" Sarah came in with a wave of energy.

"What's up?" asked Bryant as Sarah tossed the same bag of soccer balls to the floor again.

"I've been working on this new storytelling project." Sarah briefed him on her conversation with Maria and her Master Plan. Bryant was pumped at the thought of his playgrounds coming to fruition.

"How can I help?"

"Well, I need names of potential storytellers. They could be current kids or families who are thriving in the after-school program, or they could be kids who've aged out and gone on to do other things in our community. I've got this list from StoryFind of what to look for as you're thinking about people." She passed Bryant a sheet of paper.

"I've got, like, five kids who immediately come to mind!" said Bryant enthusiastically.

"That's awesome!" Sarah said. "I want to challenge you on one thing though. The StoryFind Process said to make sure we look past the usual suspects. Sometimes the more outgoing voices are the ones who have told their stories so many times that the emotion may be gone from it. So, as you're thinking of people, or asking your team to think of people, will you mention to them to look for the quieter voices in addition to the kids who will more naturally come to mind?"

Bryant nodded that he understood. Sarah continued, "If it's not too much work, do you think you could send me a little summary on three to five students? Maybe who they are, what their involvement has been, and why you recommend them?"

"Absolutely. Thank you for taking on this fundraising project! It's such a huge need, and I'm sure we'll come up with a great list for you."

Sarah was walking back to her office feeling great when Carol charged into the hallway, causing her to take a couple of steps backward. Carol was director of special projects for KidsKan, which practically meant that she ran the Thanksgiving dinner boxes and Christmas store. "Can I speak with you for a moment?"

Sarah had been lost in her own world thinking about the potential for this video and felt a bit jarred, but she said, "Sure!" and ducked into Carol's office.

Carol wasted no time in getting to the point. "I heard you're doing a video for the KidsKorner program. While I'm sure they need funds, too, I wanted to remind you that Thanksgiving is coming quickly. We typically ask for support for our dinner boxes right about now. We always have to cut corners, and funds are so tight. Why would you jeopardize dollars that might come in for my project by asking our supporters to give to something else?"

Sarah's magical world of storytelling was crashing down around her. "I don't think that will happen," she said, trying to maintain her composure.

"I think that is exactly what will happen," Carol replied, not breaking eye contact with her. "I understand you have Maria's support for this, but I'm just asking you to be sensitive toward the fact that I need the donations to be able to do my work. Would you please consider adding an ask for the Thanksgiving dinner boxes as well?"

"First of all, I understand where you are coming from, Carol," started Sarah as she reminded herself to lead with empathy. She knew that acknowledging someone's feelings or point of view always helped a situation, as it let them know they had been heard. "You have had to work so hard to make sure that our community members are able to have happy Thanksgivings. I understand the challenges that you've faced with fundraising, particularly because we haven't been able to share our stories in the past. I think we've been fundraising for you with one hand tied behind our backs."

Carol seemed to soften with Sarah's understanding. Sarah continued, "We've also stopped fundraising for the after-school program altogether over the last couple of years. It's the program that started this organization—our heart and soul. It's what drew most people to support KidsKan in the first place. There are always special things we are trying to raise support for—like Thanksgiving and Christmas—but I believe we need to kick off our storytelling by getting back to the core of what we do."

"But why can't you also add in an ask for the Thanksgiving dinner boxes?" wondered Carol.

"Because the donor will have to make a choice, and in making a choice, they are more likely to not do anything at all. Our efforts will be divided. But I'll tell you what. Let me get this story off the ground, and I promise I will tell a Thanksgiving dinner box story next."

Carol smiled. "Thank you! I'm sorry I ambushed you. I think we are all going to fight for your time and efforts over the next few months as we finally get to share our stories with the world!"

Sarah smiled and left feeling a little off-balance but also satisfied in knowing that she navigated that situation well. She coached herself to focus and stay the course. She would ask Maria to cast a vision to the whole team about what they were doing with storytelling so that everyone had a shared understanding. She had maintained her composure with Carol, but she did not want to have that same conversation a dozen more times with her other colleagues.

The next two days passed a little more slowly as Sarah waited on storyteller names to come in from Bryant. While she was waiting, Sarah read up on what she would be doing next.

According to StoryFind, her next task would be to set up Discovery Interviews with each of the potential storytellers. She learned that these were to be long, open-ended interviews with the goal of story exploration. She wanted to walk away with answers to the following questions about her storytellers:

- What is their story?
- How do they connect to the Master Plan?
- Can they display emotion?
- Does their story contain unique details that an audience will remember?

Sarah was ecstatic when she finally heard from Bryant on Thursday afternoon. In addition to program graduates Celeste and Stephen, Bryant sent over a list of three current students (Isabel, nine; Hunter, twelve; and Noah, six) who the staff felt fit the StoryFind criteria.

As soon as Bryant's list arrived, Sarah set about scheduling the Discovery Interviews. She reached out directly to the graduates Celeste and Stephen via text since they were over eighteen years old, and then she made phone calls to the parents of Isabel, Hunter, and Noah.

StoryFind talked a lot about managing expectations with storytellers so that their feelings wouldn't be hurt if their story was not selected. She was thankful to have a strategy, and she simply told each of the potential storytellers that KidsKan was gathering stories of how the organization had impacted their lives and wondered if they would be willing to sit down with her to tell their story.

By Monday, she had heard from three of the five storytellers—Celeste, Isabel, and Hunter—and had scheduled time to meet with each of them that same week. Two of the Discovery Interviews would be in person and one via Zoom, as Celeste was a couple hours' drive away at college. Sarah let each of them know that the interviews would be recorded for note-taking purposes, and they were all comfortable with that.

With actual Discovery Interviews lined up, Sarah felt exhilarated. She could not wait to hear her first official stories in person.

Maria peeked her head into Sarah's office just as she was reveling in her thoughts of her upcoming interviews.

"How's it going?" she asked Sarah.

Sarah brought her up to speed with the three Discovery Interviews she had scheduled.

"Oh! Isabel is an interesting candidate," Maria said. "Actually, what comes to mind most when I think about her is her physical activity. She is always going a hundred miles an hour! There could be an interesting angle there with her need for a playground."

Sarah grinned. "I was actually just about to come see you. Did StoryFind talk at all about Discovery Interview questions? Because I don't see anything specific in the binder you gave me. I think I can naturally come up with a few, but if they offer any guidance, that would certainly be helpful."

Maria jogged back to her office without saying a word and returned with her cell phone. "I actually snapped pictures of these very slides from StoryFind's presentation!"

Maria sent Sarah the picture of the Discovery Questions slide and then zipped off to a meeting. Sarah looked at the photo of the slide and read:

DISCOVERY INTERVIEW QUESTIONS

- Tell me your story.
- How did your story impact you emotionally?
- What is something you want people to know about your story?
- How did our organization help, and what would it have been like if we hadn't been there?
- Anything else you would like me to know?

Sarah decided to take this template and personalize the questions a little bit, while still leaving everything as broad as she could. Leaving it open-ended would allow her storytellers to be explorers of their own stories without Sarah's agenda tied to every question.

She wrote three sets of questions with the StoryFind template serving as the base and sprinkling in some specific questions about the facility and playground. Celeste's interview would be slightly different because she was a graduate of the program and able to speak as an adult reflecting back. For Isabel and Hunter, she wrote questions both for the kids and their mothers who would be accompanying them to the Discovery Interviews.

After about an hour's work, she had the following questions drafted on her computer:

QUESTIONS FOR GRADUATE (CELESTE)

- Tell me your story.

- How did your story impact you emotionally?

- What is something you want people to know about your story?

- Do you remember how you first were introduced to KidsKan?

- What were your favorite things about it?

- Do you remember playing on the playground? Can you tell me any impact it might have had on you?

- How did KidsKan help in your life?

- What would it have been like if we hadn't been there?

- What are you doing now? Did KidsKan have an impact on you going to college?

- Anything else you would like me to know?

QUESTIONS FOR PARENTS

- Tell me your family's story.

- How did your story impact you emotionally?

- What is something you want people to know about your story?

- Do you remember how you first were introduced to KidsKan?

- As a parent, what are your favorite things about it?

- What does Isabel/Hunter talk about the most when she/he comes home?

- Does Isabel/Hunter talk specifically about the playground? If yes, tell me more.
- How do you think KidsKan has impacted Isabel's/Hunter's life?
- How has KidsKan impacted your family?
- What would it have been like if we hadn't been there?
- Anything else you would like me to know?

QUESTIONS FOR KIDS (ISABEL/HUNTER)

- Tell me about what you do when you come here to KidsKan.
- What is your favorite thing about KidsKan?
- Can you take me through an afternoon here at KidsKan? What do you do when you get here?
- What do you think of the playground? Do you play on it?
- What would you want other kids to know about Kids-Kan? Should they come here too?
- Anything else you would like me to know?

Satisfied with her list of questions, Sarah felt prepared to tackle her very first Discovery Interviews. She took a moment to reflect on how much had changed over the past week. Seven days ago, her morale had been so low that she had been pursuing other job opportunities. She marveled at how invigorated she felt with her new pursuit, and she hadn't even heard the stories yet. It seemed she was as excited about the StoryFind Process as she was about the prospect of sharing KidsKan's stories with the world!

Conducting KidsKan Discovery Interviews

Sarah's first Discovery Interview was with Celeste, a twenty-one-year-old woman who projected a sense of deep determination underneath her gentle exterior. Sarah learned that Celeste was a senior at a nearby university studying political science. She had recently been accepted for early admission into her university's law school and dreamed of coming home to serve those in the community she had grown up in. She was bubbly and full of life. Her time at KidsKan taught her that she was capable of doing big things. As far as the playground, she actually remembered the first one being built. She was able to speak with emotion about how she and her friends felt they finally had somewhere to hang out that was safe and, she mentioned, beautiful.

Sarah left the conversation with Celeste in tears. She couldn't believe that this little organization could have set someone's life on a totally different path. And, of course, there was the added bonus that Celeste had actually been there when the first playground was built, and she could talk about it with emotion? Wow. This was more than Sarah could have hoped for.

The next Discovery Interview was with Isabel ("Isa") and her grandmother, Pilar. Pilar had officially adopted Isa two years prior. Pilar was in her fifties, impeccably dressed, and soft-spoken. Her eyes sparkled when she talked about Isa. Isa was beautiful, bright, and bursting with physical energy—just like Maria had said. They were meeting in a rec room, and Isa wasted no time running back and forth with a kickball.

Pilar was incredibly articulate about KidsKan. The program had given her granddaughter a sense of community and an outlet for her abundance of energy. As a grandmother, she articulated that KidsKan meant safety, help, and family. She found ways to get invested herself and was always bringing the neighborhood kids to various programs. She teared up a little bit when she told her family's story. It was full of tragedy and overcoming, and they were just now starting to find solid ground.

Sarah called Isa over and found the nine-year-old to be overflowing with joy. She loved the playground and said the girls had a secret club that would meet underneath the slides. What she really loved, though, was the organized games and sports. Her leader, Francis, had connected her to a local soccer league, and she was excelling. She was thankful to get to come to some place "cool" and "fun" each day after school.

Sarah found Isa's joy contagious, and she walked away once again astounded by the impact of the work they were doing. Pilar had expressed how thankful she was to get to share their story because she wanted others to experience the blessing of KidsKan just like her family.

It would be another two days before her interview with Hunter and his mom, Angela. Hunter brought a book and sat quietly beside his mom. Angela looked tired. Her husband was in the military and currently deployed overseas. Three days a week, she worked twelve-hour shifts as a nurse at a nearby hospital. KidsKan, she said, gave her the ability to help provide for her family.

Angela had a harder time opening up, and Sarah felt uncertain about how to help her feel more at ease. She was sure there was so much more to the story that Angela wanted to share, but Sarah wasn't sure what to do beyond asking her list of questions.

As Sarah turned her attention to Hunter, she found an incredibly articulate twelve-year-old. He was not only intellectually advanced but emotionally as well. He had two younger siblings and talked about how he had seen them come alive at KidsKan. His six-year-old sister especially loved the playground, and he talked about how proud he was of her for the friends she had made. Sarah commented about what an amazing young man he was.

Leaving the interview with Angela and Hunter was a different experience than the other two. Though Angela was guarded, she couldn't rule them out because there was something indescribably vulnerable about Hunter. He was someone you were innately drawn to and wanted to be around because you could sense his genuine care and concern for those around him. It was a remarkable gift and rare to see so on display at the young age of twelve.

How was she ever going to choose? Sarah decided to meet with Maria to process through the storytellers. Maybe Maria would have some wisdom for her on how to choose the right one.

KidsKan Storyteller Selection

The next afternoon, Sarah scheduled an hour with Maria.

"Maria, you will not believe the three amazing interviews I've had this past week," Sarah said, diving right in. "I want to tell you all about them! I know the StoryFind binder you gave me has selection criteria, but how can they possibly know who to choose? Isn't it just an instinct thing? I conducted three interviews, and they were all so good in different ways."

Sarah was quiet while Maria looked at her computer. She wondered what she was thinking and why she hadn't responded. Then in true big-picture Maria fashion, she said, "I actually think it would be good to connect you with StoryFind directly, Sarah. I'm forwarding you an email now with their contact information. They will be a valuable partner in the years to come. You're doing a great job with these small projects, but I would love you to work with them to produce our year-end campaign video this year. They have an online portal with all of the information in the binder and more. And if you're up for it, they also host in-depth training several times a year, and I'd love to send you."

Sarah couldn't believe her ears. How had so much changed in two short weeks? Her burnout job was rapidly becoming her dream job.

"You have no idea how excited I am about everything you just said. Yes to working with them on our year-end campaign, and yes to attending anything else I can get my hands on! I want to process it more, but I don't want to miss why I wanted to talk with you. Do you mind if I pull up the worksheet on selecting the right story and work through it with you?" Sarah asked.

Maria smiled and agreed. Sarah took a moment to find the right one. As she glanced at it, she could see it was divided into two sections: Round One Selects and Round Two Selects.

Under Round One, there were three criteria listed:

- Displays warmth and emotion
- Demonstrates storytelling ability
- You personally connect with

"So," said Maria, "let's see if there is anyone who naturally falls away after round one. Displays warmth and emotion. Is there anyone who did not fit this category?"

"Well, probably Hunter's mom, Angela. I struggled to get her to open up. I love Hunter, but I don't think he could carry the story on his own."

"What about the second category? Demonstrates storytelling ability?" Maria asked.

"One hundred percent Celeste. She is a natural storyteller. Pilar and Isa did a great job too. Maybe they needed more prompting, but there was enough there. Once again, I'm thinking Angela didn't do as good of a job as the others did naturally."

"Seems like we're off to a good start," Maria encouraged. "Okay, so the last one: who did you feel like you had a good personal connection with?"

"I'd say Celeste and Pilar and Isa. This is so hard! I hate not saying Angela and Hunter, but I want to be true to the process here."

"Okay, so round one is done. Is there anyone we can eliminate?" asked Maria.

"I think based on these results, we should not use Angela and Hunter for this initiative," Sarah said slowly but decisively.

"Look at our progress!" marveled Maria. "Let's dive into round two." Maria read the criteria: "Our storyteller aligns with our goals, aligns with the audience, and drives the One Big Idea with clarity."

"My Master Plan!" Sarah said excitedly. She had forgotten about it in the midst of all the storytelling excitement. "Let me grab it." She ran to her office and returned with her laptop.

As they looked at who might align with their goals, connect with their audience, and drive their One Big Idea with clarity, a winner emerged. The goal could have been reached by either storyteller, but the target audience is what really sold Sarah on choosing Celeste.

Written in the Master Plan, it said the audience was made up of "individuals who care deeply about systemic change in our community and believe that creating that change starts in childhood. People who care deeply about the safety and development of our community's children. They are motivated by seeing real change and feeling like they are making a difference."

Celeste's story encompassed everything the KidsKan audience cared about.

She was an all-around success story. She was someone who could remember the first playground being built, and she had overcome tremendous odds thanks to the help of a safe place, which was KidsKan. And on top of it all, she was planning on coming back to the community to do great things.

As excited as she was about choosing a winner, Sarah also felt like she still had two other amazing stories that needed to be told. An idea was forming in her mind. "Maria, what if we do the video around Celeste's story, and then follow up over the next two months with two written stories about Pilar and Isa, and Angela and Hunter? Those would take fewer resources as I think I could actually use the Discovery Interview content as a start for the stories. I could call them with any follow-up questions."

Maria excitedly agreed. Always thinking about operations, Maria urged Sarah to start a filing system of the stories right away too. "Make sure you store each story with a date, description, and notes of any use or potential future use."

Sarah nodded and headed out the door. In addition to the filing, she knew her next step was going to be contacting Celeste to see if she would be interested in filming her story. She texted Celeste right away and received an enthusiastic "Yes!" in reply. She said she would happily drive home from college for a day of filming sometime over the next couple of weeks.

Sarah was on cloud nine as she drove home that night. She was eager to see what the next step in the StoryFind Process would hold!

Application: The Story Hunt

My hope for you is that, like Sarah, you have direct access to your storytellers. That's always easiest, right? But if you don't, hang in there. I'll help you through that as well. We often work with organizations, grantors, foundations, etc., whose stories come through indirect sources. Don't despair! I'm here for you too.

You already hold your Master Plan in your hands. Remember that it contains everything you hope to accomplish in telling a story. Now it's time to start finding the story that aligns with your plan and will move your audience to action.

Your Storyteller List

How are you going to find your story? It all starts with an initial list of names. Sit down, clear your mind, and start coming up with a list of people you think have a story to tell and can tell their story in the most emotionally compelling way.

In the KidsKan story, Sarah reached out to Bryant because he knew the program participants better than she did. If you aren't connected to the storytellers in your organization, that's okay! Reach out to your frontline workers and arm them with a summary of your Master Plan and criteria of what to look for in a story. Ask them to share any names with you and make a personal introduction if possible.

If you are someone who works through other people or organizations, the creation of your initial list may take a bit more time. We work with a large organization that funds medical research. Their best stories are those of the patients who have benefited from the research done by the physicians that the organization grants money to. Challenging? Yeah, just a little. We had to rely on the physicians who had received funding to supply us with patient names and hospital systems that were willing (or not so willing) to let us contact their patients. It took time, but the end results were beautiful. We conducted many Discovery Interviews through the process and came back with a reserve of amazing storytellers, both physicians and patients.

I want you to remember: you *have* stories. Sometimes it just takes time to access those stories. If you feel the disconnect between your role and the frontlines, this is the time to start creating relationships with those who can connect you to your storytellers. Sometimes your road in may be a little untraditional. Maybe it will require some education for members of your team. (Remember, Sarah waited years for access to tell KidsKan stories!) It will definitely require patience and building trust. But in the end, it will absolutely be worth it.

Let's get back to creating your list of names. Warning! The initial names who come to mind may not be your best, most influential storytellers. Often, the most outgoing or most outspoken people come to mind first. They are probably very open about why they love you and your organization so much, which is great! The caution comes in that this group has probably shared their stories repeatedly. The processing and reprocessing of what they've been through and how your organization has helped could mean the emotion may not be readily available when you sit down to capture their stories.

It's also very true that some of the quieter voices may have a more significant impact on your audience. Perhaps they are the ones people would least expect. Almost always, they are the ones who aren't asking for much and display a quiet gratitude. Your organization's impact may even be unexplored except for in their own hearts. Push yourself to look past the "usual suspects." You may be surprised at what you find.

What do you look for in this initial list? People who:

- Trust you
- Demonstrate vulnerability
- Can display emotion
- Make you think, "I bet there's more to this story"
- You like interpersonally

Let's expand upon each of these a little bit. We'll combine trust and vulnerability because they go hand in hand. *Merriam-Webster's Dictionary* defines trust as "assured reliance on the character, ability, strength, or truth of someone or something." Vulnerability is defined as "capable of being physically or emotionally wounded, open to attack or damage."

If you are telling someone's story, it is imperative that they trust you enough to know that even as they open themselves up to the potential of feeling pain, their story is being well taken care of. If a storyteller does not yet have that trust in you, they are opening themselves up to potential harm or even revictimization.

On the flip side, a compelling story requires a storyteller who is willing to go to vulnerable places. Vulnerability is what connects us to the hearts and minds of others. Therefore, trust and vulnerability are the top two things to look for when searching for a story.

A note on revictimization: your organization might exist to help those who have been through something incredibly hard. For example, in the KidsKan story, some of the families lacked resources and had difficult lives they did their best to balance. Poverty, food instability, abuse, systemic failure, and trauma are sometimes part of a participant's experience, even if it isn't apparent.

You are there to make sure this person has support on their journey. We have one client whose storytellers have been through so much trauma that they have a counselor on site when stories are being told. Most of you won't fall into the camp of needing to make sure a professional therapist is present, but I want you to understand the seriousness of what you are asking someone to do. Make certain that the person whose story you are telling has come far enough along that the telling of their story is an act of empowerment. They need to be ready to use their story to help those who are coming along behind them.

You may be asking the question, "How do I know if I am revictimizing someone?" It often comes down to your own instincts and heart motives. Of course, there are goals attached to the stories you are telling, but make sure your motives for telling a story are in the right place. Your number one priority is taking great care of your storytellers. This comes before any other goal.

If at any point in an interview, you feel your motive shift to getting something from a storyteller that a donor might respond to, you've moved into potential revictimization territory. So back away, check your heart, and move forward with the storyteller's best care in mind rather than your donor's wallet.

Here are some revictimization warning signs:

- You see someone struggling to recover from deep emotion.

- You see a glazed look come over someone's eyes. (If this happens, ask, "Where did you go? Do you feel safe?" and then take a break.)

- An interview doesn't end with a true sense of hope.

If you sense revictimization, immediately connect your storyteller with support and do not, under any circumstances, use the interview.

Let's get back to the process. You started your list by thinking of people who trust you and can be vulnerable. The next thing to ask is who can display emotion. You intuitively understand this. People connect to emotions; this is what it means to be human. If a storyteller comes across as "everything is okay and always has been," there will be nothing for your audience to relate to.

An audience responds best to a storyteller who takes them on a complete emotional journey. Their words and emotions should be visibly congruent. This means their expressions are in harmony with the story they are telling. We worked with a doctor who routinely saw a lot of death based on the types of patients she treated. As she told one particular story of a recent loss, our director noticed she kept smiling at the ends of her sentences in order to mask the pain. It was clear that there was a lot of unprocessed grief. We were able to realize through her Discovery Interview that her lack of congruence might be confusing to a viewer, and that she may not be ready to share this particular story. All this to say, as you work on your list of potential storytellers, you are looking for people who can take an audience on an emotional journey while also experiencing personal healing through the telling of their story (and not more trauma).

Next, as you are looking for potential storytellers, try to think of people who you have a natural curiosity about. Who have you walked away from and thought, "I bet there is more to this story"? If you leave an interaction wanting to know the rest of the story, that is a great person to put on your list. If you are intrigued, your audience will be as well.

And finally, plain and simple, look for people you feel positive toward. If you like them, your audience will likely like them too!

Trust, vulnerability, emotion, intrigue, and likability: it may seem like a tall order for an initial list, but this truly is the best recipe for telling an impactful story.

If you are telling one story, your initial list should have about five names on it with the goal of conducting Discovery Interviews with at least three people. We typically say that the amount of Discovery Interviews you conduct should be about double the number of voices you want to include in your final piece. This gives you a great shot at finding your absolute best storytellers.

Conducting Your Discovery Interviews

The initial list of storytellers you build is for the purpose of conducting Discovery Interviews. Discovery Interviews are long, open-ended, and do not go too deep emotionally. They help you uncover a lot of valuable facts and information about your storytellers, including:

- What is their story?
- How does their story connect to the Master Plan?
- Can they display emotional vulnerability?
- Does their story contain unique details that an audience will remember?

Let's look at each of these. What does it mean to discover someone's story? Sometimes you will sit down to do a Discovery Interview only to realize that someone's story isn't what you thought it was. For example, StoryFind went overseas to capture stories for an international nonprofit. Part of its mission is serving orphaned children through children's homes. I sat down to conduct a Discovery Interview with a young man whose story had reached me via three or four different parties—meaning it had been told and retold until it finally reached me.

What I thought I was sitting down to hear (the story of a boy whose family had been murdered) was something very different (both of his parents had died of medical complications). Meeting him helped clarify what his story was, if we chose to tell it. This is one of the reasons to ask open and broad questions. I could have started with something specific like, "Tell me about the day your parents were murdered," but (apart from being incredibly insensitive) there would have been an immediate disruption of trust and a whole lot of confusion on his part. Through open-ended questions, we were able to discover what his story actually was.

The next thing you will learn from a Discovery Interview is the story's connection to your Master Plan. As you saw with Sarah, Discovery Interviews help you uncover a wealth of beautiful stories. Most of them will be set aside for later use. As you wrap up your Discovery Interviews, you will be able to determine which story best aligns with your target goals, your audience, and your One Big Idea.

Next, Discovery Interviews help you see which storytellers can display emotion. If it wasn't evident in the list-making stage, the Discovery Interview reveals which storytellers are able and willing to display emotion and which are not.

Finally, you will learn whether or not a storyteller can express their story in a way that contains unique details that an audience will remember. As much as possible, dig for details in the Discovery Interview. Look for stories with unique perspectives or quirky details that an audience can immediately visualize.

Remember Desirae from the introduction? The one who got cold feet? When she was in high school, her guidance counselor told her she was "not college material" and to get a job at the local sewing factory. Listen to that detail: "You aren't worth it. Take a job at the sewing factory." Can you feel its weight? It tells an audience exactly what her counselor thought of her potential. A job at a sewing factory might be great if that's what you want to do, but to Desirae, she was being told that it was all anyone could see in her future. Look for these unique details that can enhance your stories. Desirae's story remains one of our most beloved today because of her ability to share profound, visual details.

Conducting Discovery Interviews can feel a little intimidating. Let's think back to Sarah. She created her Master Plan, drafted her list of names, prepped questions, and went in fully prepared. You can do this too! Reach out to your initial list of storytellers and ask if you can hear their stories. Managing expectations of how someone's story might be used is tremendously important. Instead of mentioning a project or initiative you are working on, say that you are reaching out to gather stories of impact from your organization. You would like to hear their story, and would they be willing to share? This allows you the freedom to simply listen without wondering if you will hurt their feelings if you decide to go another direction.

Set aside an hour for a Discovery Interview, and plan to record your conversation. When possible, meet in person, and if you are able, record the interview using video. You can record audio alone, but you'll miss out on some nonverbal body language that may help you as you shape your story. I understand that meeting face-to-face is a luxury, so recording a video session through an online platform also works and is effective.

We will talk more about this in our interview techniques chapters, but recording the Discovery Interview frees you from note-taking responsibilities. When someone is taking notes, the person is reminded that you are studying them. A natural filter of protection kicks on in the storyteller's mind when they realize you aren't engaged in the conversation.

I remember in college, I sought out a counselor for my anxiety. I was so nervous as I walked into her office. The room was tiny, and we sat only about three feet from one another. She had a little desk directly to her left. As she asked me questions, she kept her body turned to the desk and spent the entire session looking at a piece of paper where she was fastidiously taking notes. What was she writing? What did she think of me? I never went back. There was no human connection.

Honestly, storytelling happens best when it is direct and face-to-face, when someone can receive real-time body language feedback from you, when they can sense that you care and that your only agenda is to listen.

Recording your Discovery Interviews allows you the freedom to simply be. You'll have everything captured to review later.

Let's talk through the Discovery Interview questions together. Like Sarah, you'll want to arrive at your Discovery Interview armed with questions and an openness to allow the storyteller to guide their own story. Discovery Interview questions are much broader than the questions you will ask during an actual interview.

Here are some sample questions to get you started:

- Tell me your story.
- How did your story impact you emotionally?
- What is something you want people to know about your story?
- How did our organization help, and what would it have been like if we hadn't been there?
- Anything else you would like me to know?

Let's look at the prompt "Tell me your story." There is no better way to start a Discovery Interview than to give the storyteller license to put their story into their own words. You will learn what they value, what pieces of their story they claim as important, the characters who have impacted their journey, and what they value emotionally. You can interject with supplementary questions and redirect rabbit trails as needed, but ultimately this is an exercise in a type of free association. Your job is to listen, validate, and act as a guide. Discovery, discovery, discovery!

The next question you'll dig into is "How did your story impact you emotionally?" There are layers to a person's story, which we will talk about in Chapter 6. Some people are very emotionally available, but for those who aren't, don't be afraid to ask directly how a person's journey impacted them emotionally.

Emotions in a Discovery Interview present a tricky challenge. If someone shares all of their emotion about a situation in a Discovery Interview, it may be difficult to recapture it during the actual interview. I preface my questions by letting people know I won't take them too far down emotionally and that today is simply about hearing their story. If I sense that something might be too heavy for the moment, I'll help bring them back out of it. This sets a precedent for not appearing uncaring if I cut the emotion off.

The technique I most often use for managing emotion in a Discovery Interview is simple redirection. You can do this by asking a question that is a bit off topic: "Wow. Thank you for sharing. I know that was a lot. Now, you said you had a daughter. What is she up to these days?" This subject shift jars the brain into needing to process something new, which shuts down the emotional reaction. If you're uncomfortable shifting topics so quickly, you can also suggest a quick break. When you return, ask a more lighthearted question on a different topic.

After you have captured the initial story and their emotional reaction to it, another question you might ask your storyteller is "What is something you want people to know about your story?" Ultimately, you are searching for the meaning in someone's story, not just the emotion. This is a great question that reveals how they make sense of everything. The responses you will get often have tones of "I want people to know that I am stronger today than I was five years ago. I did the work it took to get here, and I am so proud of the person I am today."

It is a beautiful opportunity for you to learn what they value most from their journey. It can also lead to unique story details that you wouldn't have known otherwise.

Once you are done hearing the personal side of the story, don't forget to ask, "How did our organization help, and what would it have been like if we hadn't been there?" This is the all-important question. You want to ensure that your organization somehow fits into their story's narrative. I have encountered people who have phenomenal stories but may say, "Oh, sure, your agency helped, but it was just a piece of my success." You want people who can sing your praises loud and clear. The connection between their story and your organization must be apparent.

Finally, end your Discovery Interviews by asking, "Is there anything else you would like me to know?" This allows for a lot of aha moments. There are always details that come to light during this time. It is your storyteller's chance to fill in any gaps of their story or to let you know anything else that is important to them.

Like Sarah, feel free to also add your own questions to the mix. These base questions, along with any others you write with your goals, audience, and One Big Idea in mind, will help you conduct purposeful Discovery Interviews.

Of course, the ultimate goal in conducting Discovery Interviews is to lead you to the storyteller or storytellers you will be using in your project. Therefore, the final piece of the Story Hunt is to select your storyteller.

Your Storyteller Selection

You've finished your Discovery Interviews, and you're ready to select your storyteller. As you saw with Sarah and Maria, there is actually a systematic approach to choosing the best story from the bunch. At StoryFind, we like to take our storytellers through two rounds of selects.

In the first round, look to keep storytellers who:

- Display warmth and emotion
- Demonstrate storytelling ability
- You personally connect with

Essentially, are they likable? Were you drawn to them emotionally? Did they tell their story with clarity and detail? Keep any of these individuals. Everyone else can be put on the shelf for now.

The second round is all about the Master Plan. Which story aligns best with your goals? Which story would your target audience be most drawn to? Which story helps drive your One Big Idea with clarity? Typically, your front-runners emerge simply from taking them through each of these filters.

If you were communicative up front with your potential storytellers, no one will be expecting you to use their story one way or another. Regardless, be sure to thank everyone for their time. Then ask your chosen storyteller or storytellers if they would be willing to share their story for whatever purposes you have outlined.

For the rest of your storytellers, we recommend creating a filing system that allows for easy access to their stories in the future. Be sure to save your recordings with a description, date, and any ideas on how you might like to use their story at a later date.

Conclusion: The Story Hunt

Finding and selecting your best stories is the second step in the StoryFind Process, and conducting Discovery Interviews is the way your frontrunners emerge. My goal in this chapter was to help you gain the tools to find your best storytellers with confidence, strategy, and purpose, so let's review together what we discussed before we move on to step three. You learned how to:

- Create a list of potential storytellers
- Conduct thorough Discovery Interviews
- Select the best storyteller for your project

Now that you have a storyteller in place (and they've agreed to it!), it's time to shape your story into something beautiful!

CHAPTER 4

ORGANIZE YOUR STORY

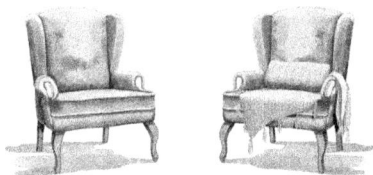

Using familiar language
subconsciously allows a
storyteller to feel comfortable
and right at home.

ABOUT FIVE years into our marriage, my husband and I decided to actively try to have a baby. We hadn't been preventing pregnancy; it just hadn't happened. We married young and had ambitions that we were both living out. We traveled a lot. Our lives were full, but we didn't feel like our family was complete. It was time, we decided. The first year was full of eager anticipation—when would it happen? Could we announce it with cute Christmas onesies? That came and went. Okay, some maybe Valentine's Day announcements? Nope, not then either.

Midway through year two, hope turned to nerves. I began buying those drug-store-brand ovulation kits that always made me feel shy at the checkout. Not sure why. Trips to my doctor assured me that everything looked normal; it just hadn't happened yet. Finally, after two active years of trying, we visited a fertility clinic. It was test after test, I could try this drug or that drug, gain weight, lose weight, destress my life (what?), sleep more, work out more, work out less, etc. I felt like my world was spinning so fast, and I still didn't have a baby.

I know you all can relate to something being right for you or not right for you. Sometimes it's a gut thing, or if you're like me, you believe it's a God thing. Neither of us felt that pursuing in vitro fertilization was right for us. We hit a standstill. Life was consumed with hopelessness and fear. It was dark and lonely. Until one day, we met a woman who asked us to adopt her baby. She was determined it was the right choice for her life and for the baby's life. She stands by that today, and we have an amazing relationship with her. My infertility gave me the gift of raising another woman's child, and our daughter is the joy of all of our lives.

Now this isn't a story I tell at parties. But it's a big life story, and worth telling. Of course, the rest of the story belongs to another woman, who was brave and courageous, and to our daughter, whom we are committed to walking with through the hard journey of adoption. As a disclaimer: I know adoption can be messy. The trauma of their losses (birth mom and our daughter) doesn't exist so that my pain can be healed. But it is my honor to walk this road with them, and this is my story.

What happens when you ask a stranger to tell *their* story—to you and maybe also to a very large audience? Remember we talked about vulnerability? Opening up to the possibility of harm? I wrestled with putting this story in because I know modern adoption can mean a lot of things to a lot of different people. I don't know what you think about adoption, and I'll be honest, I want to overexplain so you understand everyone's hearts in the situation. Your storytellers are going to feel a lot like me: a bit scared and exposed. They will want to overshare (or undershare). It will be your job to take their story, take great care of it, and shape it into something beautiful.

In this chapter, I am going to teach you how to organize a story in two ways: a simple Story Arc and a more complex Story Flow. As I have taught story organization over the years, I've noticed this part seems to overwhelm people the most. I promise I've simplified it so much, you will be able to do this with your stories in your sleep! I started this chapter with a story of my own because I want to show you how easy this can be before we dive into the thick of it together. Take my story above. It has a challenge, a struggle, and a resolution.

Challenge: We wanted to have a baby, but couldn't.

Struggle: We tried various methods and nothing worked.

Resolution: We were asked to adopt a baby and are so thankful and honored to have walked this road.

You can organize your stories just like that, so that you know what your final product will look like before you even get to the interview. As with everything else, this level of intentionality means your result will be a purposefully told story designed to help you achieve your goals and drive results.

In this chapter, we will specifically look at drafting a Story Arc or Story Flow, discovering emotional touchpoints, and drafting interview questions. My story may have raised some emotions for you, and I want that to serve as a reminder to you that storytelling (and collecting) is very personal. What may feel like simply part of your job duties will not feel that way to the person opening up to you. They are taking a big risk in sharing. And what they share might open up big emotions in you as well. So please take care of yourselves too. Secondary trauma is a very real thing.

As always, let's watch Sarah organize her story first, and then we'll walk through the process in more detail together.

The KidsKan Story: Organize Your Story

With her storyteller selected, Sarah decided to press pause and get fully up to speed on what StoryFind recommended for the next stage of the process. She settled in and began reading all of StoryFind's material on story organization.

Sarah would have to choose between creating a Story Arc or a Story Flow to organize Celeste's story into a cohesive narrative. As she read on, it looked like StoryFind suggested using a simple Challenge, Struggle, Resolution format for the Story Arc. Organizing her story this way would ensure her audience was taken on a journey—hopefully one that concluded with their own heroism as they took action in response to characters in the story.

A Story Flow seemed a little more complicated, with a few approaches suggested for writing this way: Linear Narrative, Nonlinear Narrative, Quest Narrative, and

Viewpoint Narrative. Sarah read that this type of structure would help her create clarity and focus in the story she was telling. It would also help her prepare interview questions and even work to shape the final edit of her story.

As she studied each of them, she decided that the best approach for her first attempt at storytelling was the most straightforward and the one that made the most sense to her brain. This approach was called Linear Narrative Story Flow: a story presented in the order it actually happened.

With her direction determined, Sarah's next step was to watch her Discovery Interview with Celeste. She had recorded it via Zoom, so the process of watching and taking notes would be easy. StoryFind suggested that she look for the following two things:

- The natural flow of the story in chronological order
- Any emotional touchpoints

As she watched the interview, Sarah decided that since this was her first attempt at constructing a Story Flow, she should focus on the structure first and then watch a second time for emotional touchpoints. She smiled as she pushed play, eager to watch everything unfold for the first time.

Celeste's Discovery Interview started out in the present with a lot of talk about college and her admission into law school. There was certainly some inspiring content.

In a blank document, Sarah wrote down *Current Life* and then *Law School* below it. After that, the interview went back to Celeste's time at KidsKan. She focused on three different things during her time there: the playground being built, her first memories of KidsKan when she was in elementary school, and the various people she met who inspired her along the way.

In her document, Sarah added the following with some context:

TIME AT KIDSKAN

- First KidsKan Experience
- The Playground Being Built
- The People Who Inspired Her

Celeste's Discovery Interview then moved into her life before KidsKan. She described her family: she had two half-brothers who were older and out of the house before she started at KidsKan; her father and stepmother were in and out of the house in her younger years, and they had since left the community.

Because of the neglect she had endured, she was in foster care by the time she was six years old. It was her foster mother who had introduced her to the program. She was a single mom who worked from 10 a.m. to 7 p.m. and thought KidsKan might be both a positive influence and an inexpensive means for childcare. When Celeste was nine, she was reunited with her biological mother and continued to attend KidsKan.

Sarah jotted down *Early Childhood*, *Foster Home*, and *Reunification with Mother* on her list of high-level topics as well.

The final part of the Discovery Interview focused on Celeste's hopes for the community. She was committed to work as an attorney in foster care and adoption, and she might run for office one day. With this in mind, Sarah typed out *Hopes for the Future of Our Community*.

At the end of the list, she added *Overall Impact of Kids-Kan on Celeste's Life/Where She Would Be without Us*. She knew instinctively that this would be an important piece to tie everything together. She also wanted Celeste to talk about the work that was left to be done, so she also added *The Ongoing Need for KidsKan*.

Sarah arranged her list of topics chronologically to fit the Linear Narrative structure. It looked like this in its final form:

EARLY CHILDHOOD

- Foster Home
- Time at KidsKan
  1. First KidsKan Experience
  2. The Playground Being Built
  3. The People Who Inspired Her

- Reunification with Mother
- Current Life
- Law School
- Overall Impact of KidsKan on Celeste's Life/Where She Would Be without Us
- Hopes for the Future of Our Community
- The Ongoing Need for KidsKan

All in all, the first pass through the Discovery Interview and organizing the timeline took Sarah about an hour. She felt proud of her ability to quickly construct a chronological flow of Celeste's story—especially when the Discovery Interview bounced around a lot in time. As she read through her document, she knew she had the structure in place to tell an amazing story.

Sarah decided to wait until the next day to look for her storyteller's emotional touchpoints with fresh eyes.

As the morning dawned, Sarah hadn't stopped thinking about Celeste's story. She had already begun to form a preliminary list of things she felt sparked emotion in Celeste. She went through her morning routine lost in her own thoughts. As she sipped her coffee, she grabbed a sheet of paper and jotted down some of her initial ideas about the emotional parts of Celeste's story. She came up with the following:

- Entering foster care—particularly the uncertainty she felt
- Her passion around why she wants to come back and serve the community
- What KidsKan meant to her

Celeste had either cried or lit up with joy discussing each of these. Sarah knew there was plenty more emotion; she just couldn't remember what sparked it all off the top of her head. She hurried through the rest of her routine so she could get to the office and dive into her second pass through the Discovery Interview.

As she drove to work, Sarah reminded herself that StoryFind talked about the importance of looking for subtle, unexplored emotions. They said to watch for facial cues or avoidant answers to questions as clues that something might be happening beneath the surface.

Sarah knew her goal wasn't to coerce Celeste into talking about anything that she wasn't ready to, but she also wanted to give her the opportunity to fully share her heart. Her goal was to protect Celeste and her story, while also giving her the chance to heal through the sharing of her story for the benefit of all those coming along behind her.

As Sarah slid into her desk chair and opened her computer, she didn't even check her email or impulsively open her social media accounts. Instead, Sarah immediately clicked play on the Discovery Interview for the second time.

As the interview opened with Celeste talking about her current life, Sarah noticed that Celeste shyly deflected any feelings of joy or accomplishment surrounding her admission into law school. She would glance down or change the subject quickly. Sarah knew there was more there to draw out. She jotted down *Admission into law school* on her emotional touchpoints list. She never would have thought of that on her own.

As she continued to watch, there were two more areas of emotion that really stood out to Sarah. The first was when Celeste talked about her very early childhood with her father and stepmother. She seemed to talk about it very matter-of-factly, but when Sarah listened closely, she could tell there was more there—a nervousness and dismissiveness that seemed to conceal a deeper emotion.

Celeste had also mentioned very briefly that she had met her best friend, Presley, on her first day at KidsKan. She lit up with joy talking about Presley; she even remembered them watching the playground being built together. It was such a short part of the interview that Sarah had forgotten about it.

She added everything she discovered from rewatching the Discovery Interview, and her final list of emotional touchpoints looked like this:

- Early childhood with father and stepmother
- Entering foster care—particularly the uncertainty she felt
- Meeting Presley and watching the playground being built together
- Admission into law school
- Passion to serve the community
- What KidsKan meant to her

StoryFind suggested that there might be three to six emotional touchpoints in a Discovery Interview, so Sarah was pleased that she was right on track. It had actually taken a lot out of her. It took intense focus to watch for Celeste's nonverbal cues as much as her verbal cues. While Sarah was proud of her work thus far on her Story Flow and the emotional touchpoints, she was ready to concentrate on some of her other work for the remainder of the day. She found that stepping in and out of the story helped her see it from a new perspective each time.

Drafting KidsKan Interview Questions

The next day, Sarah sat down with her StoryFind materials, but she decided that she should first check in with Celeste and make sure she was still on board with everything.

"Hello, Celeste! It's Sarah from KidsKan. How are you?"

"Hey, Sarah!" Celeste said excitedly. "I'm good! I was just thinking about you and wondering when you'd like to film."

"That's exactly what I'm calling about," said Sarah. "I'd love to schedule something over the next couple of weeks, but you let me know if there's a day that works best on your end."

They talked logistics for a couple of minutes and were able to get a time and place scheduled for the filming.

"I also want to talk through your story, if that's okay," Sarah said.

"Of course!" said Celeste.

"I organized it chronologically into a Story Flow," said Sarah, and she read Celeste the list. "Is there anything in there that makes you feel hesitant or is inaccurate? I'd love to know so we can talk it through together."

Celeste paused. "It's not that I am uncomfortable with sharing my life before foster care. I just want to make sure that we don't overly focus on it. I still love my father and want the best for him even though I haven't seen him in years. I'm definitely comfortable with talking about it, just not much."

Sarah agreed. "That makes total sense. I think the total length of our video will be three to four minutes, so we'll have a lot of ground to cover in a short amount of time. And I promise to let you review the final video for approval before it is shared with everyone. If there is anything in the final product you're uncomfortable with, I'll make sure it isn't part of it."

Celeste breathed a sigh of relief. "Thank you! I know my story is in good hands. By the way, can I see the questions you'll be asking me?"

Sarah was prepared for this one because she had read about it in StoryFind's materials. "So, I've learned that when interview questions are shared ahead of time, it seems like people start to prepare what they think are the 'right' answers rather than simply speaking from their hearts. I am going to be drafting questions that target each of the Story Flow points I read to you earlier. Would it be okay if I just sent the Story Flow your way rather than specific questions?"

"That makes sense, and yes, that would be really helpful," said Celeste. "Anything to calm the nerves!"

"All right, I'll send it right now. Thank you again, Celeste, and I look forward to seeing you next week!"

With everything scheduled, Sarah sat down to write her interview questions. StoryFind's materials included simple and helpful techniques. They said to write open-ended, non-leading questions and to include the emotional touchpoints. Each question should serve a purpose toward the video's goal and advance the storyline in some way. They also said to use the storyteller's own words and language from the Discovery Interview when writing the questions if possible. Sarah also learned she would be writing more questions than she would actually ask.

As Sarah wrote, she used each piece of the Story Flow as a guide for the questions that would be written underneath. The hardest part for her was making sure her questions didn't lead Celeste too much one way or another. A happy surprise for her was discovering that StoryFind was right! She could use Celeste's own words to create questions. She was interested to see how those questions would make Celeste feel in the interview.

In the end, Sarah's questions looked like this:

Note to self: start with casual chitchat. Ask her questions about her trip here or something simple.

EARLY CHILDHOOD

1 Tell me what your life looked like before you entered foster care.

2 Who did you live with?

3 Can you describe your home to me? What did it look like? Feel like?

4 What do you want people to know about your time there?

5 If you had to use a word to describe this time in your life, what would it be?

FOSTER HOME

1   What happened that led you into foster care?

2   Do you remember what you felt when you learned you weren't going back home? (Emotional touchpoint: a lot of uncertainty. Explore this.)

3   Tell me about your time with your foster mom.

4   What do you want people to know about your time there?

5   If you had to use a word to describe this time in your life, what would it be?

TIME AT KIDSKAN

First KidsKan Experience

1   Who introduced you to KidsKan? (Foster mom)

2   Describe what KidsKan is in your own words.

3   Do you remember your first day? What did you think? Feel?

4   Who did you meet that first day? What does that person still mean to you today? (Emotional touchpoint: meeting Presley.)

5   In our first meeting, you said you finally felt like you took a big breath of air. Can you tell me about that?

The Playground Being Built

1   We talked about how you remember the playground being built at KidsKan. What specifically do you remember?

2   What did it mean to you that you had something beautiful that was yours? (Her words about the playground from Discovery Interview.)

3   If you close your eyes, can you take me back to the day you remember running out to the playground to play for the first time. What do you see? Hear? Feel?

4   What did having the playground come to mean to you over the years?

The People Who Inspired Her

1   Tell me about the people you met through KidsKan—particularly a mentor who inspired you or believed in you.

2   What did it mean to you to have this person in your life?

REUNIFICATION WITH MOTHER

Note to self: maybe only need a couple of sentences about this.

1   When were you reconnected with your biological mother?

2   How did having KidsKan help you transition out of foster care and back home with her?

CURRENT LIFE

1 Tell me about your life now.

2 What do you want to be when you "grow up"?

3 Why?

4 What does giving back to your community mean to you?

LAW SCHOOL

1 So, you were accepted for early admission into law school? That is a huge deal! Can you tell me about this? (Emotional touchpoint.)

2 That is a huge accomplishment. What does it mean to you?

3 Tell me specifically what you want to do with your degree.

OVERALL IMPACT OF KIDSKAN ON CELESTE'S LIFE/WHERE SHE WOULD BE WITHOUT US

1 How did you get from your scared six-year-old self to where you are today?

2 What would life have been like for you if KidsKan hadn't been there?

3 What did KidsKan mean to you? (Emotional touchpoint.)

4 What do you want people to know about your journey?

5 Can you tie where you are now back (in part) to the construction of a playground?

HOPES FOR THE FUTURE OF OUR COMMUNITY

1 What do you wish for our community?

2 What do you wish for the kids and families who live here?

3 How does KidsKan support those wishes?

4 How do you want to make an impact in our community going forward? (Emotional touchpoint.)

THE ONGOING NEED FOR KIDSKAN

1 Why does KidsKan need to exist?

2 Are there others out there like you? Who benefits from what we do?

3 If you were speaking to someone thinking about giving, why would you tell them it is important?

4 Anything else you want people to know?

Sarah was so proud of her interview questions. The list was long, but Sarah believed that with Celeste naturally answering a lot of them, the entire interview should still only take an hour. She took a lunch break and returned with fresh eyes to review her Master Plan and then reread the interview questions to make sure that they aligned with the project's overall goals. Her goal was to raise funds to build two new playgrounds at a cost of about $150,000. She was certain her questions would demonstrate the value of the playgrounds to donors.

Her target audience was individuals who care deeply about systemic change in the community and believe that creating change starts in childhood. They are people who care deeply about the safety and development of the community's children. They are motivated by seeing real change and feeling like they are making a difference. She knew that Celeste and her story would deeply connect to her audience's heart.

Finally, Sarah looked at her One Big Idea: "Playgrounds are key to creating healthy children." As she glanced back through her questions, she decided that she should ask Celeste some more targeted questions about the playground. She added the following under *The Playground Being Built* section:

- What do you think is the value of a playground for creating healthy children?
- What did you learn by playing on the playground?
- How was the release of physical energy important to you or to your friends?
- Why do you think a playground is important for future kids coming through the program?

In the end, Sarah was glad she looked back at the Master Plan so she could ensure that she not only told a great story, but one that would actually serve an important purpose.

She sat back at her desk and read through her questions one last time. She was truly proud that she had a highly organized interview that would help her both care for Celeste and accomplish her overall goals.

Writing the Story Flow, finding her story's emotional touchpoints, and drafting her interview questions all took time, but she was certain they would lead to a story that people wanted to hear and would respond to.

Application: Organize Your Story

As you just discovered from Sarah, once you've selected your story, it's time to organize it into a cohesive flow. This step is often overlooked, and sometimes I hear clients say, "We'll just find the story in the edit." Please don't do that! You may find *a* story in the edit, but will it be *the* story? Will it be the one your audience is compelled to watch from beginning to end? That will move them to act?

Find your story in the Discovery Interview. It will ensure you are on the right track to achieve all of your goals and desires. You'll be surprised at how easy the rest of the process is after you've worked to create this structure.

Oftentimes Discovery Interviews—with all of their rabbit-trailing goodness—result in the need to find the story within the story. You'll walk away thinking, "That was good, and I have a massive amount of information, but which parts must my audience hear?"

So, let's break it down together. Organizing your story occurs in three parts: creating a simple Story Arc or Flow, identifying emotional touchpoints, and drafting interview questions.

Story Arc

Start by watching or listening to your Discovery Interview, and organize a Story Arc or Story Flow. Which one you choose is largely based on personal preference and your own organizational style. Feel free to play around with both and see which connects with you best. Creating this structure ensures that you know your story inside and out before you step into an interview. It also helps you create clarity and focus in the story, and it even shapes the final edit of your interview before you've even conducted it!

I want to introduce an incredibly simple Story Arc. It is the one I demonstrated earlier in the chapter. Peter Guber, author of *New York Times* bestseller *Tell to Win*, said the seminal elements that make a story great are as basic as a challenge, struggle, and resolution.

In order to tell a story that holds your audience's attention for its duration, you must first clearly identify the challenges, struggles, and resolutions in the stories you are considering telling. All stories have these elements in common, whether they are an entertaining tale told over dinner, meant to fill an exciting memoir, or deeply resonate on screen or in print and represent your organization and show its value in a personal way.

The challenge is the first phase of the Story Arc. You can set up the challenge simply by stating the problem or having a storyteller introduce an undesirable obstacle they must overcome.

The struggle is the next phase of the Story Arc. This is an excellent opportunity to connect deeply with your viewers' hearts, as this is when you're letting them wrestle with the challenge you have presented. Peter Guber said this is the phase in which you give your audience an emotional experience by narrating the struggle to overcome the challenge or find the answer to the opening question. Please, please, please do not leave out the struggle portion of your stories. If you are not comfortable entering into the struggle with your storyteller, find someone else who is. This is the most direct I will ever be in this book because it is that important. The struggle *is* the story. Without it, there is nothing for your audience to care about or respond to.

I want to give an example from an organization that does a great job of narrating the struggle in their videos. The mission of charity: water is to bring clean and safe water to every person on the planet. In one video, they present the challenge: "This community has never had fresh water." Then we experience the struggle: "The village citizens can't get the equipment needed to dig a well because a big trench separates them from the rest of their country, and there is no bridge big enough to transport the equipment. What are they going to do?"

The bulk of the video is about the struggle, as sharing vivid details of the pain that an individual or group might be facing can go a long way to deepen the connection between your audience and your organization. They hold off on introducing the hero until later, which gives the viewer a chance to feel deeply for the problem they are being asked to help solve.

Resolution is the final stage of the Story Arc. Peter Guber described this phase as when you galvanize your listeners' response with an eye-opening resolution that calls them to action.

It's sometimes tempting to think that if we leave the viewer sitting in the pain of the struggle, they'll be more likely to act. But in reality, the opposite usually happens. When someone experiences a story with no clear call to action, they are more likely to simply ignore it because they feel overwhelmed. "Why help? It's never going to improve anyway."

Resolution can be conveyed in many different ways. It could be by painting a picture of what the future holds if your organization continues to expand its mission. Or maybe the individual who just shared their struggle now shares how their life has improved because of the services you provide.

There has to be balance in the resolution. Yes, there is hope, but there also continues to be a great need—one that you need the viewers' help to solve. End your stories with the idea that there is still so much more work to be done.

Organizing your stories into a challenge, struggle, and resolution format ensures that your audience will go on a journey—a journey that concludes with their own heroism as they take action to enter your story.

Story Flow

Let's shift to a Story Flow. In the purest sense, a Story Flow is how you envision your piece will look in its final form. It is essentially an outline or a more detailed version of a Story Arc.

Within each type of Story Flow, a Story Arc is present. However, using a Story Flow allows you the most comprehensive overview of your story and ensures that the details you want to cover will come forth during your interview.

As outlined by the staff at MasterClass, there are four types of narrative story flows: Linear Narrative, Nonlinear Narrative, Quest Narrative, and Viewpoint Narrative.

Linear Narrative is what you expect: a story is presented in the order it actually happened.

Nonlinear Narrative presents a story that might jump around in time, using flashbacks or other storytelling techniques to take the reader on a journey that is not chronological.

Quest Narrative has a hero on a relentless quest toward a specific destination. They face obstacles and challenges at every point along the way that they must overcome to obtain the prize.

Finally, Viewpoint Narrative expresses the point of view or subjective personal experience of your storyteller. This might mean someone writing their own experience for your newsletter, or you receiving permission to write it from their perspective. It allows for a lot of unique details to emerge and remain unfiltered.

Each type of narrative presents opportunities to keep your audience interested in the stories that you share.

As we journey through the creation of a Story Flow, I want to share an example from one of our clients, CCV International (real name changed to protect anonymity).

We work with their development department, and they put on live events for current and prospective donors a handful of times each year. They asked us to tell a donor story, rather than the typical recipient story, to inspire others to recognize that their giving matters too.

Our company chose to tell the story of Warren and Brenda Pfohl. They were not the most likely candidates—self-described "failed missionaries" who did not have many resources when they started giving. They were recreational and occupational therapists, turned missionaries to Poland, turned caregivers to their son who, after thirteen years, passed away from a fatal progressive illness, turned major donors to CCV International.

After their Discovery Interview, we decided a Linear Viewpoint Narrative would be the best approach to tell the Pfohls's story. This is how we arranged their Story Flow:

- Current Family (light topic to start off)
- Warren and Brenda's Relationship Backstory
- Faith Backstory
- The Beginning of the Journey
- Moving to Poland
- Transition Home

- Losing Their Son
- First Fundraising Event
- Giving Journey
- Why ccv International

It may seem simple to organize a story in this way, but most of the time, Discovery Interviews are a bit messy and all over the place. In our hour-long call with the Pfohls, we hopped around from topic to topic and back and forth in time. In the end, it was our job to organize the major events and milestones to give the story shape.

If you are wondering how the Story Arc fits in, we actually chose to start this story with normal everyday life. The challenge entered the picture during the Poland section, where health concerns required the Pfohls to return to America as self-described "failed missionaries." The struggle came in the Transition Home and Losing Their Son sections. Hope started to form at the First Fundraising Event and in their Giving Journey. Finally, resolution and clarity came through the Why ccv International section.

The beauty of giving a project a Story Flow structure is that it usually stays largely intact through the actual interview and you can use it to guide your final edit.

Emotional Touchpoints

After you've given your story some structure, it's time to identify emotional touchpoints. As you watch your Discovery Interview, identify areas that seem to generate emotion in your storyteller and make note of them. Remember, Discovery Interviews do not always explore the fullness of someone's emotions, so you may have to look for subtle hints that emotion is present.

With the Pfohls, we identified the following emotional touchpoints:

- The loss of their son
- That God would use them to give
- Returning from Poland broken

After identifying potential emotional touchpoints, we wrote questions designed to specifically draw out these emotional touchpoints. Here is what Warren and Brenda said during the actual interview when asked what it was like to return home from Poland, having lost their careers as missionaries:

Warren: We thought we would be missionaries the rest of our lives.

Brenda: That was a very defeating time for us.

Warren: (voice wavering) I felt like a failed missionary. I literally felt like God had just grabbed me by my hair and just flung me and said, "I hope you do well," and walked away.

Deep emotion is written on Warren's face as he describes what he felt as deep abandonment. This is the power of being prepared. We see raw humanity emerge. None of this was present in our first interaction with the Pfohls in the Discovery Interview, but because we could see that it *might* be there, we were able to draw it out on interview day.

So, look for potential emotion and write questions that help your storytellers fully explore that emotion.

Write Interview Questions

After drafting your Story Arc or Story Flow and identifying emotional touchpoints, sit down and write your interview questions. Your Story Flow should serve as your outline for writing questions. Each question should serve a purpose toward your goal.

Here is a peek at a few of the Pfohls's interview questions. We simply took the Story Flow and drafted interview questions to support and draw out each topic.

CURRENT FAMILY

- Tell me about your family.
- Tell me the story of how the two of you met.
- Was it love at first sight?
- What did Warren look like then? (Humorous moment in the Discovery Interview.)
- How did you finally get together?

RELATIONSHIP STORY AND THE BEGINNING

- How long have you been married?
- Did you always feel called to ministry?
- Brenda, did you feel a call overseas?
- Warren, what did you think when she said she felt called to be a missionary?

POLAND

- How did you receive a call to move to Poland and plant a church? (Their own words from the Discovery Interview.)
- What was it like to leave everything behind?
- What was your time there like?
- Did you give monetarily even as missionaries?

TRANSITION HOME

- Why did you come home?
- What did you feel when you came home?
- Warren, where did you end up working?

As you write your questions, make sure they are very open-ended. Do not ask questions that yield yes or no answers, but rather allow the storyteller to explore and express their own thoughts and feelings. Most of your questions should not be leading, which means you are not trying to force your storyteller toward the answer *you* desire. You're allowing them to explore their own reality. We will touch on skillfully using leading questions in Chapter 6.

Write way more questions than you will ask. In fact, write down everything you might want to know for each section of your Story Flow. When you walk into an interview, you want to know the story you are telling inside and out (to the best of your ability). The act of writing questions cements the story in your mind. You will likely only use a fraction of the questions you've prepared, as your storyteller will naturally answer them as they tell their story. But if they don't, you'll be ready to serve as a very prepared guide.

Use the storyteller's own words and language from their Discovery Interview. For example, the question "How did you receive a call to move to Poland and plant a church?" was taken directly from Warren saying "We received a call to go to Poland to plant a church" in his Discovery Interview. Using familiar language subconsciously allows a storyteller to feel comfortable and right at home.

Finally, make sure you've included plenty of questions about the emotional touchpoints you have identified. As you will learn in our Interview Techniques chapter, sometimes drawing out emotion happens in layers—the first question you ask might not elicit the emotional response you hoped for. Don't be afraid to circle back to the topic until you are confident that their emotion has been thoroughly processed.

Conclusion: Organize Your Story

Whew! Do you feel prepared to step into your interview? I know this organizational work takes time, but I think you'll come to see the beauty in finding the story early. There is a tremendous amount of freedom that comes from being prepared and knowing that when you sit down with your storyteller, you will absolutely get what you need to share an impactful story.

Let's review together. After reading this chapter, you can:

- Choose and create a Story Arc or Story Flow to give your story shape and structure
- Use the Discovery Interview to identify emotional touchpoints in your storyteller's story
- Write great interview questions using your Story Arc or Flow as a guide

The next two chapters are my favorites. We are going to explore how to actually conduct an amazing interview during which your storyteller feels loved and taken care of. Because the two chapters are focused on the same event—the actual interview—we only visit the KidsKan Story at the beginning of Chapter 5. Chapter 6 continues the application of the process. Are you ready? Let's dive in!

INTERVIEWER
FUNDAMENTALS

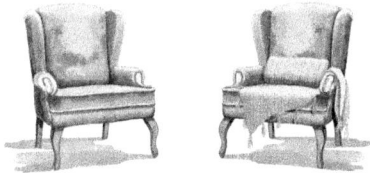

Remind them about
the lives that will be changed
because of their willingness to do the
hard thing and be vulnerable.

T THIS point on your StoryFind journey, you are well down the path of telling a great story! You have found the one that fits best with your Master Plan, decided how you want to tell it, and drafted your interview questions. All of this will serve you well, but there is one last thing to work on before you actually capture your story: interviewing with skill, the fourth step in the StoryFind Process.

Interviewing is one of my greatest passions. It is a delicate art form that, when done right, leads your storytellers to a state of pride and your audience to a place of action.

There is a lot at stake in an interview. I have had the honor of working with organizations that tell extremely challenging stories. I spent my thirtieth birthday in Nepal interviewing girls who had been rescued from sex trafficking. My thirty-fifth birthday was spent interviewing severely injured war veterans. I've had the privilege of interviewing homeless youth, terminally ill cancer patients, and scores of others in between. Each person's story deserves to be treated with respect and dignity.

You don't have to be as passionate as I am to conduct a great interview, but you do have a personal and ethical responsibility to know what you are doing before you sit down and ask someone to open up to you. The next two chapters will teach you how to do two things: interview well and take great care of your storyteller.

Let's walk through Sarah's story, so you can see how she does it before we dive into learning technique.

The KidsKan Story: Interviewer Fundamentals

The day had come: interview day! Sarah drove herself to work, half paying attention to the road and half reviewing Celeste's story over and over in her mind. She knew she should give herself grace with this being her first interview, but she was feeling pressure to get it exactly right. The butterflies in her stomach made it feel like she was heading to her first day at a new school.

After writing her interview questions, Sarah had spent the days leading up to interview day learning techniques and tips on interviewing from StoryFind. She felt ready to apply as many of them as she needed, and she was really glad she had prepared such thorough questions ahead of time. They felt like a safety net that she could rely on to get great story content even if everything else she had learned fell flat.

An hour later, Sarah was standing at the entrance to KidsKan watching as Celeste pulled into a parking spot. She put on a warm smile and, taking her cue from Celeste who was walking up with her arms open, gave her a big hug. Maria had wanted to be there, too, but Sarah asked her to stop by afterward. StoryFind talked about having the interviewer be the only point of contact with the storyteller before the interview, taking care not to overwhelm them with too many people to talk to.

"Welcome back!" Sarah said happily. "How are you?"

"Thank you! I'm good. Very nervous," responded Celeste.

Sarah started to say "Don't be nervous!" but caught herself, wanting to validate Celeste's feelings and not shut them down (a StoryFind technique she had learned). After all, what could be more intimidating than realizing you are about to share your story with not only one person but an entire audience of donors? Instead, Sarah responded, "The nerves make sense. What you are doing today takes a lot of courage. I promise I will do everything I can to help you feel comfortable. And if at any point you need a break, you just let me know. You are in total control of your story."

Sarah had chosen a quiet spot for the interview. It was simple, and the audience would be able to see the playground through the window. As they wound their way back to the interview room, Sarah walked Celeste through what to expect.

"I hired a local production company, so when you walk in, I will introduce you to Paul and Jeff. Paul is running the cameras, and Jeff is helping with lighting and sound.

"Oh!" Sarah paused as they passed the restroom. "Would you like to freshen up a bit before we go in?"

Celeste said yes, and while she was getting ready, Sarah grabbed them each a bottle of water. When Celeste emerged, they headed together to the interview location chitchatting about the lingering summer weather.

As they entered the room, Paul and Jeff said hello. Sarah made quick introductions, but she kept her focus on creating trust with Celeste and helping her feel comfortable. There were two cameras set up with different angles. A chair for Sarah sat next to the wide-angle camera, and Celeste's chair was about six feet from Sarah's chair. Most of the gear was set up already, and Sarah explained to Celeste that she could grab a seat in her chair while Paul and Jeff did final tweaks to the cameras, lights, and sound.

While the final adjustments were being made, Sarah took a seat in her chair opposite Celeste and set her questions on the floor next to her. She wanted to minimize the feeling of this being an interview. As much as possible, it should feel like a casual conversation. Sarah had to trust that she had done the work to shape Celeste's story and that she knew it inside and out. To be safe, she had spent an hour the night before going over and over the questions.

"I didn't expect to be this nervous!" Celeste said, glancing around the room at everything.

"I know it's a lot," said Sarah, leaning forward in her chair slightly in an attempt to subconsciously demonstrate relaxation for Celeste. "Once we get going, just focus on me. I will ask you questions, and you can take your time answering. I'll make sure that you are safe. If you ever feel like you don't like an answer to one of my questions, you can always answer again. We've got a whole hour blocked out, and the final video will only be three to four minutes. So, we'll edit the best pieces of your story together."

"Okay, that sounds good," Celeste replied.

"One other thing to be aware of: the audience will not hear my voice ask you the questions. So try to answer in complete sentences whenever possible," Sarah said.

"I'll do my best to remember," Celeste said eagerly.

"Well, while Paul and Jeff are finishing up and we are on the topic of college, tell me about your favorite class right now," Sarah said. She had almost started telling Celeste about a new program at KidsKan, but she caught herself just in time. She remembered StoryFind said to avoid talking about herself before the interview and instead work on getting Celeste talking casually. She aimed to roll the casual conversation right into her first interview question without Celeste knowing a transition had happened.

Sarah and Jeff had created a code earlier in the day where he would simply touch her back when they were ready to roll. Normally, Sarah would clear any excess people from the room, but both Paul and Jeff were needed to run the equipment. Proud of how she had handled getting Celeste settled into her seat, Sarah was listening to her talk about a pre-law class while also eagerly anticipating the signal from Jeff that she could start the interview.

"Okay, we're ready to roll!" Paul said eagerly.

Sarah's heart sank. Her eyes darted to Jeff, who looked at her apologetically. Paul recognized his error and said, "Oh no, I'm so sorry!"

"It's okay!" Sarah replied, trying to play it cool and gather her thoughts at the same time. Celeste looked nervous all over again, so Sarah decided to take the opportunity to remind her of the bigger picture.

"Before I ask my first question, I just want to say thank you again, Celeste," Sarah started. "Because of your willingness to be here today, so many kids' lives are going to be changed. Remember, don't hold anything back—we can always cut it later. And I know it can be tempting to censor your emotion, but your ability to share what you are feeling is what will propel people to give to this project. So as much as you can, just be yourself today, feel what you're feeling in the moment, and I promise to guide you through it each step of the way."

"I'm ready," said Celeste eagerly.

"Well, let's get started with an easy question. Tell me about your plans for the first football game this weekend! You mentioned you would be going?" Sarah said.

Celeste giggled and started chatting again, and Sarah watched as her shoulders physically relaxed. Struggling with her own nerves as an inexperienced interviewer and the slipup with Paul, Sarah reminded herself that she was going to do well today for two reasons. First, she genuinely cared about Celeste. And second, she had chosen a storyteller who already possessed a natural gift for storytelling. Sarah's job was just to help shape what she knew was already going to be an excellent story.

Sarah knew that in order to care for Celeste, she needed to practice empathy and actual listening. Sarah had learned that empathy would look like entering into Celeste's experience and feelings without projecting her own views of what she thought Celeste should think or feel. And in order to practice active listening, she would need to eliminate her mental distractions and simply be present. She would work to not think ahead to her own responses or follow-up questions.

As Celeste was talking, Sarah was also paying attention to the nonverbal communication that was happening between them. She noticed it was a little chilly in the room, and as a result, her own arms and legs were crossed. She quickly shifted her posture to a more open position—resting her arms gently on the arms of the chair and uncrossing her legs.

As Celeste finished talking about her weekend plans, Sarah knew she was ready to ask her first official interview question. She shifted slightly and leaned forward. "Tell me what your life looked like before you entered foster care," she asked softly.

"Before I entered the foster care system, I lived with my father and stepmother. I wish I could come up with something positive to say about either one of them, but the reality is they weren't around much. My grandmother, my father's mother, lived with us until I was four, and she was everything to me. When she passed away, I lost my entire sense of safety."

Celeste paused, and Sarah knew she had to press in a little bit. She was talking matter-of-factly, and Sarah knew that there was more there beneath the surface. StoryFind talked about peeling the onion in an interview—how the first time you ask a question, you'll get the response that the storyteller is comfortable sharing. The second time you press into a subject, you'll likely get a more emotional response. The third layer involves asking, "What does this all mean to you?" Sarah knew she would ask that at the end of the interview, but she wanted to see if there was another emotional layer first.

"Oh my goodness, Celeste. That must have been so hard as such a young child. If you think back to that period in your life, close your eyes and picture yourself as a little girl there, what do you feel?" Sarah asked compassionately.

Celeste sighed. "Okay, you're going to do this to me so fast?" She half joked as her eyes filled with tears. After taking a moment, she started to speak again. "When I look back at myself as a little girl, I just want to wrap her up tight and tell her that nothing happening around her is her fault. She is not bad and not deserving of the way her parents treated her. You see, my mom left me as a baby and my father remarried a woman whose children were older. She didn't have any interest in raising another woman's child. My dad had to choose: party with her or stay home with me. And more often than not, he chose her.

"My grandmother lived with us until she passed away when I was four," Celeste said again. Sarah noticed that for editing purposes, some of these second answers would be better to use. Tears were streaming down Celeste's face, and Sarah entered fully into the emotion with her and started to tear up as well.

One thing Sarah had not anticipated was the difficulty of not being able to verbally respond to Celeste. She wanted to jump in with a quick word of comfort or even a quick "hmm," but she recognized that her voice would be heard on camera. She made sure instead to fully use her nonverbal communication. Her facial expressions mirrored sadness and concern, and Sarah nodded her head thoughtfully at what she hoped were appropriate times.

"What did you lose when you lost your grandmother?" Sarah asked.

"My entire life as I knew it," Celeste said.

Celeste stopped, and her chin dropped to her chest. Sarah was so tempted to jump in and rescue her, but Celeste seemed to be wrestling with something in her own mind. One of the techniques StoryFind taught was embracing the pause. When done correctly, healing happens in these hard places of silent reflection, and at the right time, holding a silence until your storyteller is ready to speak again helps them give their own meaning to stories. Though her whole body was tensing up at the quiet, Sarah knew the most loving thing she could do was to give Celeste time to find her words again.

The rest of the time spent on her early childhood was simple back-and-forth Q and A, and Celeste seemed highly engaged in the process.

When Sarah felt they had thoroughly explored the topic, she moved on to talking about foster care. Celeste had already talked about the event that led to her placement, and the emotion had been so heavy this far that Sarah made a strategic move to talk about a subject she knew would bring Celeste back up a little bit: her foster mom.

"Tell me about your time with your foster mom," Sarah asked encouragingly.

"I know that it isn't the case for everyone, but the best thing that could have happened to me was being placed with my foster mom, Kimberly," Celeste said. "Kimberly was single and from my neighborhood, so I didn't have to go far. I hadn't really connected with a mother figure since my grandmother's death, and I felt starving for her attention, yet afraid it would go away at a moment's notice. I know I was probably a lot for her in the beginning, but she loved me without reservation and unconditionally. My heart came back to life slowly, one week at a time, maybe even one day at a time."

Sarah was excited because this seemed like the perfect moment to use the restatement technique. She knew that restatements are simply reflecting back to the storyteller what they just said using their own words. Using one here would allow Celeste to reflect with greater depth on what she had just said. It would also allow her to clarify or emphasize what might have been the most important part to her. It would also break up what was starting to feel like a monotonous Q and A interview. Sarah hoped it would leave Celeste feeling loved and understood as she could see that Sarah was listening and understanding.

"So, it sounds like your time with Kimberly was incredibly transformative in your life," Sarah said softly.

Tears formed again, but this time with a happy smile. "I honestly don't know where I would be without Kimberly. She was so steady for me. Even now, I still call her Mom. I was with her for three years until I was reunited with my biological mother."

Sarah paused for a moment before asking her next question. She wasn't sure why, but it seemed like it was the right choice because Celeste led herself right into her next topic, which was her introduction to KidsKan.

"It was actually Kimberly who brought me to KidsKan for the first time," Celeste started. "I don't know if I even had any friends before that. I was at the end of first grade, and we first came to see if the summer program would be a good fit for me. KidsKan had just moved into this building. I remember that when I walked in, it felt like school, only I belonged here a little bit more."

"Tell me more about that sense of belonging," Sarah pressed when she noticed Celeste had trailed off and was now looking at the ceiling and fidgeting a little bit. "What did it mean to you?"

Celeste sighed. "My whole life had been about survival. Even those first few months with Kimberly, before I came to KidsKan, were all about trying to adjust. I just think about myself as a little girl, and I don't know how I did it. My first day at KidsKan I actually met my best friend, Presley. She's my best friend to this day even. She lived with a foster family too. They eventually adopted her, but that's beside the point."

"You didn't feel out of place for the first time?" Sarah asked as she saw Celeste struggling with words.

"I didn't feel out of place for the first time," Celeste echoed back, nodding her head. "I had a friend and a community around me that loved and cared for me. I wasn't alone. I wasn't just trying to make it. I was ... *me* ...

a person who was worthy of being included and valued. I have many, many relationships with people I met at Kids-Kan that I will love for the rest of my life."

Sarah transitioned to talking about the playground. "Tell me what you remember about the playground being built here."

"The summer I started at KidsKan, this place was pretty empty. We had our classroom and gym, but we were basically sitting on a dirt lot. It was hard as little kids to feel like we were cooped up inside all day. I remember a guy named Mike was in charge of all the rec activities at the time."

Sarah found herself thinking about Mike. Celeste's voice was talking in the background, but she wasn't listening to what she was saying. Sarah had dated Mike for a while right after she graduated from high school and they had had a painful breakup. She had mostly forgotten him, but the mention of his name was really jarring. She realized Celeste had stopped talking, but she wasn't prepared to ask another question.

"Let's grab a drink of water," Sarah said. They both paused, and Sarah felt momentary relief because in reaching for her water bottle, she could also glance at her questions. Sarah coached herself that she could think about Mike later, but for now she needed to ask another question.

"If you close your eyes, can you take me back to the day you remember running out to the playground to play for the first time? What do you see? Hear? Feel?"

"I actually vividly remember the first day we got to play on the playground—or the fire truck, as everyone called it, because it, duh, was made to look like a fire truck!" Celeste giggled. "I remember actually feeling like the fact that it was a fire truck and not just a normal run-of-the-mill playground was something that was incredibly special to me. It was unique. It was ours.

"It was extremely hot the first day we got to play out there. It must have been midsummer because we had been anticipating it for a while. We were all being extra silly, and no one was paying attention during the designated classroom time until finally they just said, 'Go play!'

"We all ran for the door and there it was in front of us. It was real. It was ours! I remember playing for hours with Presley on that fire truck. Actually, years. We grew up with it. I think there has always been a piece of me that feels some ownership in that playground because we were the first to use it. We were the first to experience the joy that came from it."

Unprompted, Celeste went on: "I've actually been saving my own money to give toward the two new playgrounds. I don't have much, but I know how transformative it was for me to have a safe place to play—a place that was new and beautiful and, well, just mine. I want other kids to have that too. It's so important for kids like me—who may not have come from safety or from material wealth—to have a place to call their own that is taken care of. I will do whatever I can to help provide for other kids because I am so thankful that the people who worked at and supported KidsKan poured into me."

Sarah took a breath and leaned back in her chair. She watched as Celeste leaned back in hers as well. They exchanged smiles.

"I'm getting tired!" said Celeste. "I mean, I knew this would be emotional, but it's a bit like a roller coaster going back through it all at once ... There's ups and downs," she trailed off.

"Speaking of," said Sarah, trying to gauge how much energy Celeste had left. She decided to collaborate with her a little bit rather than simply going through her own agenda. "I was going to ask about your reunification with your mother, but I think that's a section of the story that we don't necessarily need for the video. Earlier you mentioned that the reunification happened, and I think maybe that one line about it is all we need. What do you think? I'll leave it up to you, though, if you'd like to talk about it today."

Celeste sighed. "You know, I think you're probably right. I feel like that is another story all on its own."

"Okay, well, let's jump ahead a little bit then. Tell me what you're up to today and what your hopes are for your future."

Celeste described her plans for law school and her aspiration to come back into the community to work in foster care and adoption and to hopefully run for office.

Sarah felt like she had been on a roller-coaster ride herself. Her ability to focus was waning a bit, and the ups and downs of Celeste's story had left her feeling a bit fatigued. She was so tempted to end the interview there, but she knew she had to practice one more StoryFind technique before everything was officially done.

Application: Interviewer Fundamentals

We'll see how Sarah wraps up the interview in Chapter 7, but for now, I'd love to take you on a journey of creating a powerful interview experience. This chapter focuses on the fundamentals of conducting an interview of your own, and Chapter 6 dives into specific techniques.

I love to study great interviewers—from Barbara Walters to Oprah Winfrey to Erin Moriarty to my own therapist. The masterful ones are so deeply connected to their storytellers that the rest of the world fades away. What creates that connection?

When I was in graduate school, we learned dozens of theories and counseling techniques. But in the end, we learned there is one key ingredient for why people change, open up, or remain stuck and closed off. That ingredient to success was the client's relationship with the therapist. This same thing applies across the board with interviewing as well: if you work on yourself first, you will go a long way in creating a relationship that invites a storyteller to open up.

Great interviewers possess the ability to:

- Create trust and put someone at ease
- Create motivation
- Practice empathy
- (Actually) listen

Let's look at each one of these abilities. Creating trust is an art, not a science, and the fastest way to build trust is by demonstrating genuine care for another person.

Some of this might be second nature to you if you are instinctively a helper, but it can be learned if you are not. I take very practical steps during every interview to ensure that the person telling their story feels loved and cared for. I want to walk you through what creating trust looks like on a production set, so you can do the same things during your interviews.

First off, if you are the interviewer, be the first person to greet the storyteller. Make casual chitchat and briefly introduce them to whoever else might be in the room. Ahead of the interview, make sure anyone else in the room knows that the storyteller should be primarily conversing with you. When introductions occur, they should reply with a brief wave or "Hello, thank you for being here," and then you take back over. You are the storyteller's best friend and guide for the day.

After introductions, ask the storyteller how they are feeling and then validate their feelings. One of the things that immediately shuts someone down is telling them not to feel a certain way about a situation.

"You feel nervous? You don't need to feel nervous! This will be so easy!" Well, no. They already *do* feel nervous, and their nerves are valid! I can think of few things more intimidating than opening up your personal story to strangers. Whatever a person responds with, let them know it's okay to be feeling it. "I can understand why you would have some nerves. This is something very few people have the courage to do. Thank you for being here today. I promise to make it as easy as possible."

Explain the process of the interview. If it is on camera, bring along support so your only job is to act as the interviewer. Show your storyteller where they will be sitting and where you will be, and explain that they will be looking at you the whole time. Keep this direction simple, brief, and warm as you guide them to their chair.

There are always some adjustments that need to take place once a storyteller is sitting in their spot—tweaking the lights, moving in the microphone, adjusting focus, etc. Use this time to put the storyteller at ease. Be the mirror for whatever emotion you want them to be feeling. For example, sometimes a storyteller will be nervously cracking jokes. Redirect them with soft responses or quiet laughter. Ask questions to help ground them in the present: "How was your drive over?" "Remind me, how many kids do you have? Tell me a little about them." Avoid talking about the actual story they will be telling, so they aren't retelling it just a few minutes later.

Also, as we learned with Sarah, don't overly talk about yourself. Talking about yourself requires the storyteller to focus on you, which may be challenging if they are battling nerves and are stuck in their head. They will expend energy they may need to tell their own story. Instead, help them warm up by talking about topics they are comfortable with or might enjoy discussing.

One time I was on set with a large international nonprofit. We were interviewing their executive director about the organization's vision for the next five years. He arrived to set totally distracted. Normally, he is a warm and friendly gentleman, but that day he was pacing and giving short answers to small talk, and the marketing director started looking nervously my way.

I pulled her to the side and asked, "What does he love to talk about?"

"Not his kids right now," she said. "They're at really stressful ages, and I know he's going through a lot at home."

"Noted! Okay, what makes him light up more than anything?"

"Oh, I know! Ask him about the first time he learned about our organization," she replied.

"Perfect." And it was! He was not expecting the question and his entire demeanor shifted. He went from preoccupied with whatever was distracting him (I still wonder about it sometimes) to engaged and full of life and vision.

Two years later, the same marketing director called me to tell me she had been studying my interviews to figure out how to replicate them herself. She said, "I have never seen our executive director so relaxed as he was that day! How did you do it?"

Laughing, I reminded her of the conversation we had had ahead of time. She was actually the one who put him at ease by knowing him well enough to know what he would delight in talking about! I simply applied it.

If your storyteller is in a weird headspace, find something you can talk about that will bring them to life before you start asking your questions. It's as simple as that.

Next, when you're ready to roll, make sure anyone who doesn't need to be in the room is seated out of sight to maintain intimacy.

If possible, do not tell the storyteller you are rolling. If your camera operator can give you a tap on the shoulder when they're ready to go, you can ease from small talk right into the interview without the storyteller's awareness. This creates confidence as they will often answer a couple of questions before they realize the dreaded interview has already begun. Little do they know, they are already answering your questions with ease!

While trust is, of course, fundamental to a successful interview, creating motivation in your storytellers is equally necessary. One of the most important things you can do before the interview begins is to remind your storyteller why they are telling their story. If they've come with any misgivings or have determined in their mind that they are going to leave out certain details or not be emotive, this is the time to remind them of the importance of what they are doing. Remind them about the lives that will be changed because of their willingness to do the hard thing and be vulnerable.

Explicitly tell your storyteller that if there is anything they are thinking about holding back, to please share it today and you can always edit it out later. Tell them if they are considering shutting down their emotions, how important it is that they be as uncensored as possible. Let them know that you will take care of them well, that you will guide them carefully through their story, and that lives will be changed because of them.

Disclaimer: In this process of creating motivation, make sure you are still honoring your storyteller's boundaries. They need to feel motivated *and* have an understanding that they are in control of what they share and that you will not push them too far. Anything they say no to should be one hundred percent respected immediately.

The third thing great interviewers possess is an ability to practice real empathy. As you sit down to do the interview, make empathy your closest companion. *Merriam-Webster's Dictionary* defines empathy as "the action of understanding, being aware of, being sensitive to, and vicariously experiencing the feelings, thoughts, and experience of another of either the past or present without having the feelings, thoughts, and experience fully communicated in an objectively explicit manner."

The storyteller is the only one who can confirm whether or not you are actually practicing empathy. Empathy is not projecting onto someone what you think they should be feeling or thinking. It is not feeling your own sadness and assuming someone else feels sadness about a situation as well, for example.

Empathy takes things a step further. It is entering into an experience with another person and feeling their feelings along with them as they share their story. Empathy in interviewing takes a lot of intentionality and a lot of focus. Because interviewing is also strategic, it's natural to think about what you want to ask next or if you're on the right track rather than being in the moment with your storyteller. But as much as you possibly can, try to stay present and attuned.

If you find yourself experiencing the same feelings as your storyteller, you're likely on the right track! I will often cry along with someone or find myself experiencing anger if I notice their intensity increasing. It's okay to state these feelings back to the storyteller as a reflection of what you are seeing. "I am feeling angry alongside you right now."

The trick with experiencing empathy is to not let it take over and become about your own story. If you find yourself on the tip of an "I know just how you feel; I once . . . ," you're on the wrong track. Watch out for those "I know" statements and never share a personal experience or anecdote during the actual interview. Afterward, sure, but not during it.

Another faux pas I see regularly is when an interviewer says, "Doesn't that just make you feel X?" Well, maybe it makes *you* feel that way, but it doesn't necessarily make the storyteller feel that way. These types of statements can shut a people-pleasing storyteller down quickly. If they are not advocates for their own feelings, they may agree with you only to later feel discouraged by the inaccurate telling of their own story.

The reality is you don't know how they feel. Even if you lived through something similar, their story has unique facets to it. And one thing that shuts a storyteller down quickly is when they feel like you've missed them. You were clicking along and then, oops, all that trust you've worked to create vanishes.

When tempted to make a statement about how you think they might feel, ask a question instead. "How did that make you feel?" Or "What were you feeling as you shared that?" Then affirm, validate, and feel that feeling along with them. Allow your storyteller to guide their own emotions, and join them in that.

The final attribute of a great interviewer is their ability to actually listen. Listening has always come easily to me, but I am aware that doing it well takes a lot of intentionality. I'm pretty quiet by nature, and I truly enjoy listening to people share their stories and experiences. I love being invited into someone else's world to process life, to share joys and sorrows, and to laugh until it hurts with them.

Listening while interviewing is vital because it makes the interviewee feel safe enough to share their story with you. If they can sense your disinterest or distraction, you have broken trust. So, let's talk about how to listen in three parts: attending, actual listening, and care.

Attending

Attending is how you orient yourself physically toward the person you are talking with.

To attend to your storyteller, make sure you maintain eye contact and engage your facial expressions as you practice empathy. Nod your head or tilt it thoughtfully to affirm your storyteller. It takes a lot of energy and can seem unnatural to consistently use nonverbal communication. But a simple smile and a nod can go a long way in letting your storyteller know you're not only listening, but you actually care.

Another form of attending is to act as a physical mirror whenever possible. Help the storyteller feel comfortable by sitting in a way that they would naturally sit. For example, if I'm with a teenager (and there's space between the cameras and the lights), you'll probably find me sitting crisscross applesauce in a chair or on the floor. I'm always leaning forward, except when they take a moment to reflect—and then I might lean back to allow them space to process. Help the storyteller know that you are safe by removing yourself as a distraction.

I've been asked, "Isn't this inauthentic? I wouldn't normally sit that way." Or I've heard, "It isn't natural for me to engage my facial expressions that much." My answer to that is yes, it might be inauthentic, but when done with the right motives, it is the highest form of love. Sacrificing yourself for the sake of helping another person feel safe is a tremendous responsibility that requires a lot of your own vulnerability; you are stepping outside your comfort zone to help create a safe space for them.

Actual Listening

Actual listening is not only hearing what someone is saying but also understanding the underlying message of what they are saying both verbally and nonverbally. Here are three simple things to remember:

1   **Eliminate mental distractions:** We're all busy. We all have a hundred things racing through our minds at any given moment. But your one job is to be in the moment with the person in front of you. You do not have to do anything else but listen to and draw out their story.

2   **Don't think about responding:** The second you start thinking about what you're going to ask next, you are no longer listening. Pause and take a few seconds to think of your next question after they finish answering if you need to, but as much as possible, be in the moment with them.

3   **Look beneath the surface:** People often feel so much more than they're saying. Try to read between the lines by watching their body language. Are they fidgeting? Are their eyes wandering? Do they have their arms crossed in front of them? Observe their choice of words. Observe their tone. And when you recognize that something is being said verbally that is incongruent with what is being said nonverbally, seek out the disconnect.

Caring

If you do none of the above and only focus on caring for your storyteller, your listening ability will go up tenfold. If you care, you naturally ask good questions, engage yourself in the content you are hearing, and are empathetic.

As you've just discovered, listening requires a lot of intentionality, but it will be greatly rewarded with a storyteller who trusts you and therefore is willing to be vulnerable with you.

Conclusion: Interviewer Fundamentals

Having the ability to create trust and motivation, practicing empathy, and actually listening are the hallmarks of the best of the best interviewers. They are also skills that can be learned and practiced! You may only conduct a handful of interviews every year, but you likely have dozens of conversations every day. All of these interview skills can be practiced in everyday life. Try them out and see what happens!

CHAPTER 6

INTERVIEW TECHNIQUES

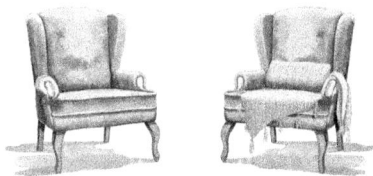

If there is one interview
skill to master, it is the discipline
of allowing moments of silence
at the right times.

N THE last chapter, you learned the fundamentals of conducting a great interview. This chapter is about applying specific techniques during an interview to help a storyteller explore their thoughts and feelings more fully. These are the skills that help an interview (or a casual conversation!) go from a Q and A session to a robust dialogue.

I want to tell you the story of my worst interview ever because I promise you nothing you face will be this bad. I need to start by saying it wasn't entirely my fault, though I accept responsibility for going along with it.

We have a client through a client, a large regional service provider that works through a marketing firm. We talk to the marketing firm and they talk to the client, you know how it goes. Well, after we chose our storyteller, the marketing firm decided they did not want the interview on camera; they simply wanted a voiceover of the story laid over some supplementary footage. No problem. They also wanted the interviews recorded in a recording studio. Kind of a problem?

I should have flagged this as something that would spike storyteller nerves, but I understood where the marketing folks were coming from. Great sound quality, right? Unfortunately, the quality of sound was the only thing that was great.

The storyteller and I were to be seated tightly together in a dimly lit room, squeezed up against a full drum kit. On one wall was a large two-way mirror behind which sat half a dozen people all staring at us (though we couldn't see them). Our chairs weren't oriented toward each other either; they were angled slightly toward the mirror so the people on the other side could see us more directly. There was also another handful of people from the client's various departments on a Zoom call so they could watch the interview. Oh, and one last thing: they asked me to wear my headphones so that I could be on a phone call with them and they could give me real-time feedback for follow-up questions.

The storyteller was nervous to say the least. I tried to relax so that he might mirror that, but the feeling of being under a microscope was so strong. I had questions prepared, memorized, and laid to the side, but new questions came in every minute or so. I had to grab a pen and jot them down while the storyteller was speaking. If I didn't write them down or decided to delay asking them, I was called out of the room into a "sidebar" to discuss why the question was important.

In the end, it was a lesson in everything *not* to do in an interview situation: remind the storyteller that everyone is watching them, take notes so they think you are analyzing them, and ask them to rephrase things every couple of minutes so they never get in the flow of actually conversing. I promise your interviews are going to be a piece of cake compared to this experience. I want you to walk away from this chapter feeling like you know exactly how to create an inviting environment and be a safe and encouraging interviewer.

Interview techniques are best learned through practical application, and not every technique belongs in every interview. My goal is to give you some tools to draw out your stories in new and interesting ways. As you become more familiar with each one, you will find most become second nature—even in your day-to-day conversations.

We are going to cover a lot, but you have my full permission to pick and choose your favorite techniques. Only use what feels natural. While some of these techniques come from the world of psychology, no interview should ever be viewed as or conducted as a counseling session. These techniques are simply ways of helping your storytellers talk about their stories from new angles. With that disclaimer in mind, here is a list of what we'll look at, and then we can break each one down together:

- Nonverbal awareness and mirroring
- Avoid interviewer mode
- Embrace the pause
- Peel the onion
- Crisis counseling
- Leading questions

Nonverbal Awareness and Mirroring

We have touched on nonverbal awareness some, but I want to make sure we cover it thoroughly because your nonverbal communication sets the tone for the entire interview. GoodTherapy.org defines nonverbal communication as "the act of conveying a thought, feeling, or idea through physical gestures, posture, and facial expressions ... Each movement and combination of movements of the body—such as shifts in posture, direction of the eyes, gestures of the limbs, and expressions on the face—provide signals to others."

After conducting two studies, Albert Mehrabian, professor emeritus at the University of California, Los Angeles, quantified communication of feelings and attitudes: he theorized that words account for 7 percent; tone of voice, 38 percent; and facial expression, 55 percent.

Think about that. We are masters at reading the nonverbal cues of others and running them through a filter of meaning. Therefore, your nonverbal cues will either put your storyteller on edge or put them at ease. If you are working with clients cross-culturally, it is also important to remember that your own nonverbal cues may mean something different to that individual.

I handpicked a list of nonverbals to be aware of in your interviews and have elaborated on each of them. As you read through them, think about your own nonverbal communication in day-to-day life. How aware of it are you? Do you use it to draw people close? Push people away? Spend a day attuned to your nonverbals and see what you think. Your day-to-day nonverbal behavior will translate into making a storyteller feel comfortable with you, so keep the following in mind:

- **Eye contact:** Maintain a comfortable level of eye contact with the storyteller.

- **Physical distance:** Place an appropriate distance between the two of you, and avoid physical barriers if at all possible.

- **Posture:** Lean slightly forward in a relaxed and open posture. Avoid crossing your arms or legs.

- **Gestures:** Avoid fidgeting and distracting motions.

- **Volume and pace:** The volume at which you speak goes a long way in putting someone at ease. If you have a gregarious storyteller and you need them to soften for an interview, modulating your volume helps to subdue their energy. Similarly, if you need someone to increase their energy, talking quicker and at a slightly louder volume can bring up the energy of an interview.

- **Facial expressions:** Your facial expressions should be relaxed, showing positive regard to the other. This is where your expressions should remain unless you are entering an emotional moment with your storyteller.

- **Tone:** Your tone should be even, natural, and calm.

Your body language is especially important if you are recording an interview on camera. You may not be able to respond verbally to something your storyteller is saying (as verbal affirmations are difficult to edit out if you are using the audio or video), but you can use your body to show that you are hearing, feeling, and attending to each part of their story. As they sense your ease, they often mirror it back to you.

Speaking of mirroring, let's look at that interview technique next. Mirroring is defined as a typically unconscious behavior where one person imitates the body language, emotions, or speech patterns of another. The scientific term for it is limbic synchrony. There is actually a set of nerve cells in the brain called mirror neurons that are responsible for this unconscious mirroring. How cool is that?

Relationally, mirroring can signal interest or attraction, and it actually demonstrates empathy! This demonstration of empathy is why the conscious act of mirroring is so crucial during an interview. It signals to the other person's brain that they can trust you.

While mirroring occurs unconsciously, we can also use it proactively to help put others at ease. Mirrors work two ways in an interview. First, remember that as you actively mirror the body language of your storyteller, the act of mirroring helps to create trust. I had a therapist once whose mirroring of my body language became almost humorous when I was aware of it. If I reclined in the chair, back he went! If I was making eye contact, so was he! Looking over at the wall, his eyes went where mine went. Ankles crossed? Yep, his too. But what he was doing was active vulnerability. He was saying, "You're in control here. I don't have anything to prove. I'm on this journey with you."

The second way we use mirroring is to help modulate or create feelings within a storyteller. For example, suppose a storyteller is nervous. In that case, you can actively adjust your nonverbal behaviors—your tone of voice, your posture, your facial expressions—to help their mirror neurons fire to follow suit and relax. If a storyteller is struggling to express an emotion fully, I might demonstrate that emotion with my own nonverbal behavior to help them achieve it within themselves. For example, there are times when my own tears have helped a storyteller be able to release theirs.

Experiment and observe mirroring in your interpersonal relationships. It is pretty fascinating! You'll find that the people you are most comfortable with are those with whom you share this limbic synchronicity. It's actually pretty wonderful.

Avoid Interviewer Mode

Our next interview technique is one I like to call "avoid interviewer mode." From time to time, I have observed interviewers go into interviewer mode, a sort of old-school thing where an interviewer acts as more of a "celebrity host" than a friend or guide. Someone says the camera is rolling, and they're "on." "Well, John, I am so glad to have you at your interview today. Let's get started with our first question."

You can still see this on shows today, like 20/20 or *48 Hours* (which I still love, by the way). That interview approach is often very different from ours as we are striving to reach different goals. On those shows, the interviewer is the authority in charge. While they may be looking to inform or expose, you're looking to share or create hope and change. Vulnerability is lost when your storyteller sees you as authoritative. If you can be on a level playing field, then trust and vulnerability will result.

Another way I see interviewers attempt to control or take charge is with note-taking. We talked about this briefly in our Story Hunt chapter (Chapter 3), but I want to reinforce it here: please do not take notes. Your goal is to keep synchronicity intact by not doing anything that might take the storyteller out of sharing their story. If you are recording your interview, there's also no need for note-taking. An interview already causes nervousness, and when a storyteller is wondering what you're writing down, it has the potential to trigger more insecurities and does nothing to put them at ease.

I have spoken with interviewers who are insistent that they are most comfortable when jotting down notes during the interview. Their reasons are always about their own comfort and not about the comfort of the storyteller. When you are writing notes, you aren't able to give your storyteller what they need to feel safe enough to fully open up to you.

Finally, set your questions aside. You've prepared and prepared for this day. You've written your Story Arc or Story Flow and drafted great questions. Now it's time to trust that you've done the work and are prepared to interview without needing them as a prompt.

One of the fastest ways to help your storyteller feel comfortable is to quickly get into the rhythm of conversation. I find that having a sheet of paper on my lap that I am glancing down at breaks up the feeling of two friends in a natural flow, and it's a reminder that there is an interview taking place.

I recommend you find stopping points throughout the interview—especially once someone is already in the mode of talking—and simply say "Let's take a quick break" to stretch your legs, grab a drink, etc. Use that time to glance through your questions and make sure you're on the right track.

I like to make a star next to anything we've chronologically missed. At the end of an interview, I pick my questions back up, go through them from top to bottom, and fill in the gaps. By this point, you're both comfortable, and it is much more natural to have that piece of paper between the two of you.

Embrace the Pause and Use Restatements

Let's talk about one of my favorite interview techniques: embracing the pause. Every Tuesday morning, I sit down with my own counselor. Having someone draw me out each week through psychoanalytical counseling has been truly life-changing for me. I have learned so much! Like clockwork, at 10 a.m., I walk through his door, recline in his easy chair, and we sit in total silence until I'm ready to speak. The first six months of this were torture, and if I'm honest, I would get angry when he wouldn't ask a question and save me from the silence. But now I look forward to it. It is a chance for the dust to settle in my mind and for me to speak when I'm ready. He does this periodically throughout our sessions too. If I trail off, he'll often just sit with me in it. When I speak again, it is with purpose and often with a new insight.

The same can be true in an interview situation, though I wouldn't recommend sitting quietly in the beginning. Dr. Joshua Schultz writes on PositivePsychology.com that if implemented skillfully, silence "can encourage clients to reflect, connect with their feelings, and continue their train of thought." I can say with confidence that if there is one interview skill to master, it is the discipline of allowing moments of silence at the right times.

This technique is the one I see interviewers struggle with the most. It is human nature to want to break up uncomfortable moments or rescue a storyteller from feelings of discomfort. But if a storyteller falls silent during an interview or you can sense that they are wrestling with a thought or emotion as they finish a sentence, simply allow them to be until they are ready to speak again. In short, do not try to fill in the gaps for them.

Healing happens in these hard places of silent reflection; meaning is given to stories; revelations are made. The most loving thing you can do is to hold the silence as sacred while giving your storyteller time to find their words again.

This technique may not be used in every interview (or more than once during an interview), but when you can sense that someone is feeling a lot—maybe after they've just shared a new revelation—simply reflect an affirming sigh or a "hmm" and wait until they are ready to speak again.

How long is too long when it comes to silence? In an interview, I typically allow about twenty to thirty seconds to pass (it feels *much* longer in the moment) before I step in and ask what they are feeling and thinking. Normally, people speak up before then, but if not, then it's okay to step in and try to help them vocalize their internal experience.

If you like the technique of embracing the pause, using restatements is another one I think you will enjoy. A restatement is a form of responding to another person by repeating, in different words, what they said, focusing on the essence of what they said they feel and what is important to them.

Okay, so that's a mouthful and a little bit confusing. More succinctly, restatements reflect back to someone what they just said using slightly different language.

There are a myriad of benefits to using restatements:

- It allows for a storyteller to reflect on what they just said, oftentimes with much greater depth
- It allows for a storyteller to make clarifying statements that may provide more detail than the initial thought
- It breaks up the flow of Q and A, which can start feeling a little too intense for some storytellers.
- It leaves storytellers feeling loved and understood as they know that you are listening and striving to understand

Practically, restatements require you to be very actively attuned to what your storyteller is saying. For example:

Storyteller: After my son died, I wasn't sure what I was supposed to do next. I felt lost and alone, like I'd never felt before.

Interviewer: It sounds like after his death, you were experiencing loneliness that was unfamiliar and uncertainty about what was to come.

Storyteller: Yes! I honestly didn't know how to put one foot in front of the other. Every day was a struggle to figure out the next thing. I just kept telling myself to do the next thing—sit up in bed, walk down the stairs, turn on the shower. The depression was dark and heavy. It's still there today. I don't know if it will ever fully lift. It's just . . . hard.

There are so many more details in the storyteller's second response. You start to gain an understanding of what their day-to-day struggle looked like with much greater depth and clarity.

Like embracing the pause, restatements should not be used more than two or three times during an interview. Sometimes they hit the mark, and you gain a wealth of new information; sometimes they result in a simple affirmation of your reflection. The greatest challenge with this technique is allowing yourself the freedom to be an active bystander in the interview. In those moments, you are not there to interject your agenda or share your own story or advice. Your job is to allow the storyteller to see their reflection and comment on it as they desire.

Peel the Onion

This leads us to my favorite of the interview techniques: peeling the onion. Psychotherapist and father of Gestalt therapy Fritz Perls viewed the unfolding of adult personality as the peeling of an onion. Knowing that there are multiple layers to someone's personality should serve as a reminder that when a storyteller sits down to do an interview with you, they are typically hiding behind some of their less authentic constructs.

The first time you ask someone about a topic that you know carries emotional weight or significance, the response you will likely get is the safe version of their story. It is the story they have told many times, often free from emotions as their minds have built protective layers around it.

During an interview, don't be afraid to return to topics you know hold emotional power more than once. The second time you ask a question or probe a topic, the response you get will often be more authentic. If you've proven to be trustworthy and they feel safe enough to go to new levels, your storyteller may start to open up as the surface layers begin to break down.

Often, this is where an interviewer will stop—we got to the emotion, yay! But there's actually a third layer that gets straight to the heart of the story and ties everything together in a way that provides meaning, closure, and hope. The exploration of this layer begins with the storyteller's answer to the question "What did this all mean to you?"

The answer to this question is often the innermost layer of content needed for the resolution portion of your story, and it's a great question to end each of your interviews.

Crisis Counseling

More than any other counseling technique, my course in crisis counseling shaped my view of conducting an interview. In both crisis counseling and interview situations, you have very little time with the person, are often dealing with weighty subject matter, and will likely not see the person for aftercare. Therefore, how you handle the interview can be a very delicate matter.

The biggest thing that stood out to me with crisis counseling is a technique I like to call doing the dip. The dip is a visual metaphor for how I view a session or an interview. Imagine a horizontal line starting on the left side of a sheet of paper representing the status quo. Each interview starts here. It's safe and grounded. We then dip down into the hard, messy, emotional, raw, real-life stuff, and then come right back up to the status quo by the end of the interview. I visually picture this line and dip as I conduct each interview, reminding myself of where we are in the process and where we need to end up.

Practically, this means organizing your questions around everyday life, questions around the trauma or the hard things, and then ending with questions about meaning-making, hope, or practicalities.

The best way to demonstrate this is through an example. We work with an organization called Homes For Our Troops. Homes For Our Troops (HFOT) is a publicly funded 501(c)(3) nonprofit organization that builds and donates specially adapted custom homes nationwide for severely injured post-9/11 Veterans, to enable them to rebuild their lives. Every Veteran who comes through the program tells their story in a video; they discuss how they were injured and what a home would mean to them both practically and emotionally. Most interviews are of both a Veteran and a spouse being interviewed together. We start by getting them talking:

Tell me how the two of you met!

This usually results in some cute, lighthearted moments—the status quo—easing them into talking to someone they've never met before.

Then we dip:

- Were you together at the time of your injury?
- Tell me about that day.
- What happened?
- What was it like getting the call that your spouse was injured?

Bring it back up slowly:

- Tell me about your home now.
- What is hard about it? (Still in some of the challenges.)
- What features are you looking forward to in a new home? (Getting the brain grounded back in practicalities.)
- What would having a home from Homes For Our Troops mean to you?

It's simple but purposeful. You are acting as a guide through what is oftentimes incredibly emotionally challenging terrain. Your job is to lead them down and bring them right back up out of it.

Leading Questions

The final interview technique is using leading questions. Leading questions are designed to elicit a specific response or to make a person think in a certain way. When you drafted your interview questions, your goal was to write open-ended questions that would allow the storyteller to explore their own stories without your influence. During an interview, however, leading questions may be used responsibly as impromptu, supplementary questions in addition to your base questions.

By nature, leading questions are influential: you are trying to lead someone to a specific response. One common interview setting where you might see leading questions is in a police interrogation as a tactic for reaching the truth: "Isn't it true that you … ?" "And isn't it also true that … ?" The same can also be said of an attorney who is trying to lead a witness to a specific response in an attempt to sway a judge or a jury.

However, when used in a storytelling setting, leading questions can act as an aid or prompt toward deeper emotion. They are most often used when you are trying to guide a storyteller to an emotion you know is present but is not being accessed. They can also be effective when you remember content from a Discovery Interview, but the storyteller is having difficulty reconnecting to an emotional place or a memory.

There are several categories of leading questions, but for your interviews, you may find yourself most commonly using these two strategies: asking for agreement and tag questions.

Asking for agreement is a technique applied by asking a very leading, closed question where you are asking the storyteller to agree with it.

- Is it true that you are happier now?

- Do you agree that you have the right to feel sad about that?

Asking for agreement, when used skillfully, can elicit some of the most emotional responses. Sometimes a storyteller needs to know that you think it is okay that they feel the way they feel. When asked with empathy and understanding, a leading question that asks for agreement can feel like the safest time to be honest during an interview.

Because these questions are close-ended by nature, if a storyteller answers with a simple yes or no, ask them to expand upon that.

Tag questions are short questions "tagged" onto the end of a statement. You state your thought or a fact and then essentially ask the person to agree with you. They include phrases such as *isn't it*, *don't you think*, and *didn't you*. Here are a few examples:

- That is a hard thing to do, isn't it?

- The weather was extra hot that day, don't you think?

- Your mother had a hard time being married to your dad, didn't she?

In a storytelling interview, tag questions are most often used as a rescue. For example, if someone is struggling with guilt or shame surrounding an issue, I'll often try to interject what I am feeling about them and help them believe the same thing by using a tag question.

One time, a soldier was struggling with guilt that his comrades passed away while he tried in vain to rescue them, resulting in the loss of "only" his legs. As he wrestled with emotion, I remember softly saying, "That was a brave thing you did, don't you think?" He looked up slowly, and there was a slight sense of relief as he realized that maybe, even though he condemned himself, the world didn't look at him the same way he did. He was able to continue the interview by exploring whether or not he thought his actions that day were brave.

As with everything else we've discussed, leading questions must be used with skillful empathy. Your goal must be to encourage and support your storyteller's own thoughts and feelings rather than impose upon them your own. When done right, leading questions can generate some of the most profound emotions.

Conclusion: Interview Techniques

All of these beautiful techniques will help draw you into a relationship with your storyteller. The outcome will be connection, intimacy, and empowerment. Your audience will be drawn in and captivated as they, too, are able to experience real connection.

As I mentioned earlier, you can use these techniques in your day-to-day life, as well as with your storytellers. What may seem awkward or clumsy at first will soon become second nature with a little bit of practice. Here is one more rundown of our whole list of interview techniques:

- Be mindful of your nonverbal communication
- Practice mirroring to elicit the emotional response you would like
- Abstain from note-taking
- Make sure you don't go into interviewer mode
- Prepare questions, learn them, and then set them aside
- Embrace the art of a skillful pause and use restatements
- Peel the layers of your storyteller's onion to get to the core
- Practice the crisis counseling dip when needed
- Use leading questions as they benefit your storyteller

As we close this chapter, I want to leave you with a final thought. It is important to note that you will not click with everyone. If you find a great story in a Discovery Interview but know that you aren't the best person to draw it out, seek out someone you think will connect with your story-teller to do the actual interview. You can't be all things to all people, and no technique in the world can compensate for chemistry that just isn't there.

In summary, the world of interviewing requires care and vulnerability on your part in order for you to most fully enter the world of your storyteller. I'm confident that you're armed with great techniques, but make sure you always go back to self-work first. Never forget that the key ingredient in a successful interview is the storyteller's knowledge that you care about them deeply. If they know this, your interview content will be amazing.

CHAPTER 7

WRAPPING THE INTERVIEW

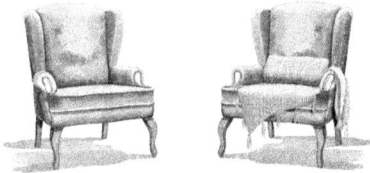

The process of aftercare
depends on the storyteller and
type of story you told.

NTERVIEWING IS LIKE running a marathon (or a half marathon, in my case. I don't know how you full marathoners do it). Mile twenty hits and you are so fatigued. The level of focus you have given to caring for your storyteller while also applying a whole lot of strategy by asking the right questions in the right way and making sure the story they're telling is accomplishing your goals—it's a lot. You will definitely not feel like doing the work to finish well.

One time, we were doing interviews for a capital campaign at a university in the heart of New York City. We conducted a location scout, asked all the right questions, but could not control the fact that construction began on a building next door on the day we arrived to film. Alumni were flying in from around the country, and rescheduling was simply not an option.

In addition to needing to connect with the storytellers and draw out the right messaging, I also had to stop the interviews every time the noise from the demolition got too loud. We were seated in a beautiful historic room with gorgeous light pouring in from the side windows, which offered a constant reminder of potential sound threats as men in green vests worked away in my peripheral vision.

The level of mental concentration it took to be attuned to each one of those things meant that by midafternoon, during interview number five, my body said it was done. I was swaying back and forth in the interview chair and almost passed out. It's the only time I have ever had to say, "I literally can't go on." We had the content, but I had no ability to do the things that make an interview end well. Thankfully, our director stepped in, I ate a banana, and all was well. I share this story so that you know you're not alone if you're feeling like everything you have to be aware of is a lot.

Another time we were filming at a stadium (not our choice of locale, but the only option available) and someone was sharing a deeply traumatic story when, I kid you not, Kenny Chesney started warming up for his concert right outside our suite. Sometimes you have control over the environment and other times, well, you just have to roll with it and be flexible. You can plan and plan, have everything in place ... and then Kenny shows up.

Conducting interviews well is a lesson in endurance, intentionality, and a great deal of flexibility. There will be times when you show up totally prepared and something throws you for a loop. This chapter's lessons are twofold. First, it gives you a system of review, a safeguard if you will, for the end of your interviews, so that even if you are dealing with mental fatigue or big distractions, you still walk away having accomplished your goals. Second, it gives you a strategy for aftercare for your storytellers, who likely will feel like they also ran a marathon.

Without further ado, let's jump back into the KidsKan story and watch as Sarah finishes out her interview, and then we'll walk through the practicalities of ending well together.

The KidsKan Story: Wrapping the Interview

Celeste had just finished describing her entry to law school and her aspirations for coming back into the community. Sarah was very ready to end the interview, and she started to justify to herself that she was sure she had what she needed. She was determined to follow the StoryFind Process through to the end, though, so instead of telling Celeste they were done, she decided to take a break instead.

"Let's pause really quick," Sarah said to Celeste, as she leaned over to pick up her interview questions off the floor. "Feel free to get up and stretch your legs, take a drink, and I'm going to look through everything to make sure we're at a good stopping point."

Underneath her interview questions was a checklist from StoryFind: the Soft Stop Checklist. It contained a list of everything she wanted to have accomplished before Celeste left that day. The list looked like this:

- Do we have all of the pieces of a Story Arc?
- Do we have each piece of the Story Flow?
- Is there anything we might want to know a little more about?

- Did the storyteller emote? If no, is there still an opportunity to capture emotion?
- Are there any places we need pickup lines?
- Are there any places where we need the storyteller to answer more concisely?
- Did they speak with clarity on how our organization helped?
- Did they answer the question "What did this mean to you?"

Sarah took each bullet one at a time. She skipped the first one since she had written a Story Flow. Then she glanced through each one of her Story Flow bullets:

- Early Childhood
- Foster Home
- Time at KidsKan
- Reunification with Mother
- Current Life
- Law School
- Overall Impact of KidsKan
- The Ongoing Need for KidsKan

"Wow," Sarah said to herself. "I completely forgot to ask her about the overall impact of KidsKan." She flipped to her interview questions and circled that section.

The next two bullets were "Is there anything we might want to know a little more about?" and "Did the story-teller emote?" Sarah thought for a moment and felt the content was solid and that almost all of Celeste's answers contained some sort of emotion.

The question "Are there any places we need pickup lines?" was next on the list. Paul had been taking note of any sound interruptions or any places where Celeste might have started to answer a question without giving it context. Sarah reached back and took his list from him and saw just one note on the sheet that said *Get a lead-in for the question "What did you lose when you lost your grand-mother?" Celeste answered, "My entire life as I knew it." Maybe have her say something like, "Losing my grandmother was more than the loss of a person."*

Sarah was grateful to have Paul's help. Next up was "Are there any places where we need the storyteller to answer more concisely?" Sarah admitted she did not have the capacity to track whether or not this was the case. She'd have to trust the editing process to tighten things up as needed.

To "Did they speak with clarity on how our organiza-tion helped?" Sarah said a confident but silent "Yes!"

And finally she saw the last bullet point read, "Did they answer the question 'What did this mean to you?'" She found herself smiling again as she realized other people, even the experts, must be prone to skipping this question.

She skimmed through her interview questions and felt confident that the only things she needed to pick up were what KidsKan meant to Celeste and then, at the end, she would grab the pickup line about Celeste's grandmother. She was sure that the five minutes she took to review the Soft Stop Checklist would help tie the entirety of Celeste's story together.

"Okay, Celeste!" Sarah said with renewed energy. "Are you ready to finish up?" Celeste was looking out the window on the other side of the room and walked back over to her chair. "I promise we are *so* close to being done, but I did forget to ask you about one important thing. I want to hear what your time at KidsKan meant to you," said Sarah. This was the final layer of peeling the onion.

Celeste's eyes instantly filled with tears. "Let me grab another drink first. This might take me a minute," she said as she held up a finger.

"Oh, I know just how you feel," Sarah said as Celeste grabbed her water. "KidsKan has meant the world to me through the years," she trailed off as she realized she was starting to talk about herself and impose her own experience on Celeste. "I'll just be quiet for now." She laughed, recovering. "Your experience is your own, and I can't wait to hear about it."

"Okay," said Celeste slowly. "My time at KidsKan meant safety. It meant friendship. It meant learning what it means to be a productive member of society. Ultimately, though, what KidsKan gave me was the ability to play and actually be a little girl."

"What did the playground mean to you?" asked Sarah.

"What your supporters need to know"—Celeste paused thoughtfully—"is that giving money to build a playground is not about play equipment. Whether or not we kids consciously understood it at the time, that playground meant that someone cared about us. They believed in us and wanted us to be our *best*. It meant safety, fun, friendship… all key ingredients to living a happy, fulfilling life. I am who I am today because of the people who poured into me at KidsKan, the friendships that I formed here, and the people who cared enough to give their time and money so that I would have a fighting chance to do something productive in my life. How can I ever thank you?"

Sarah kept rolling with the momentum. "Are there still kids who need a playground in the same ways that you did?"

"There are absolutely still kids in our community who desperately need what KidsKan has to offer. They need the programs, they need the people, and they need the playgrounds. I am proof that a playground is one aspect of making a pivotal difference in a child's life," she said with conviction. "Those playgrounds are so needed."

Celeste grabbed a drink of water and then said, "Woo, you're killing me, Sarah! I don't know how you're doing it, but here I am giving you every last ounce of my emotional energy for the day."

Sarah smiled and said, "Well, thank you for being willing to go through this process with me. You have done an amazing job. I actually have just one more thing for you today. Earlier, when I asked you a question, you answered it without context, so I just need to grab a lead into the sentence. And actually if it's okay with you, can I just give you a line to repeat back to me?"

"Absolutely!" Celeste said without reservation.

"Okay, so the question was 'What did you lose when you lost your grandmother?' I want you to just say back to me 'Losing my grandmother was more than the loss of a person.' We have the rest of your answer."

Celeste nodded. "Can you say the line again?"

"Losing my grandmother was more than the loss of a person," Sarah said directly and clearly.

"Losing my grandmother was more than the loss of a person," Celeste repeated back. "Okay, let me get myself to that emotional headspace really quick." Celeste took a moment and closed her eyes and then said the line again with more conviction. "Losing my grandmother was more than the loss of a person."

"That was amazing, Celeste, truly," Sarah said. "Is there anything else you can think of that I might have missed? Anything I didn't ask you about?"

"I can say with certainty that I cannot think of a single thing," Celeste said confidently. "Can I give you a hug?"

Sarah and Celeste both stood and embraced, and tears were in both of their eyes as they stepped back.

"You don't know what this has done for me," Celeste said. "I have always been a fighter. I don't believe in being a victim but in moving forward to make the world better. I've never had such a direct opportunity to give back before. To think that my story could impact the lives of others is just mind-blowing to me. It's an honor to be here with you today."

"I cannot thank you enough for being willing to share your story," Sarah responded.

The two women hugged again, and just like that, the interview was over. Sarah walked Celeste to her car before collapsing in her office. She was spent in every way imaginable. Her brain hurt a bit from trying to keep all of the details straight, and she was emotionally depleted from the experience. But in addition to that, she was incredibly satisfied. She knew without a doubt that Celeste's story would raise significant funds toward the two playgrounds.

A Break in the Process

Three days after the interview, Sarah was sitting in her office checking a few tasks off her to-do list before diving into a day full of meetings. The interview footage was with the production company as they organized an editing timeline. They had arranged a deal where they would edit together in kind of a hybrid fashion. Sarah was confident she could edit the story down, but she was not confident in her ability to do the more technical aspects like adding supplementary footage (B-roll) and music, tweaking color, etc. The break between the interview and editing would also give Sarah a chance to learn some of StoryFind's editing process.

And speaking of reviewing StoryFind materials, one of the tasks that she still needed to complete was reviewing their aftercare plan. She decided to look at it before her 10 a.m. meeting, which left her about twenty minutes.

Skimming the sheet, Sarah reviewed what she had learned before the interview about retraumatization or revictimization. Essentially, there were three warning signs to look for:

- You see someone struggling to recover from deep emotion

- You see a glazed look come over someone's eyes

- An interview doesn't end with a true sense of hope

Sarah had had these signs in mind during the interview and knew that Celeste had not struggled to recover from deep emotion or dissociated at any point to her knowledge. The interview had certainly ended with a great deal of hope.

Still, Sarah decided to check in with Celeste and make sure she still felt positive about the experience. StoryFind recommended a series of questions that Sarah felt were important to ask both now and again after the video had been shared. Sarah sent Celeste a quick text asking if they could talk later that day.

A few hours later, Sarah found herself back in her office and dialing Celeste's number.

"Hey there! How are you?" she asked.

"I'm good!" Celeste said cheerfully. "I'm so nervous about how this story will come together, though."

"I understand. I'm actually nervous too!" said Sarah, affirming Celeste's feelings. "But only because I have no idea how I'm going to be able to edit anything out of the video. Each piece was such an important part of your story!"

"I just keep going over it in my mind, wondering if I said enough," Celeste said honestly.

"This is totally normal, Celeste. You shared more than enough. You have no idea how many people are going to be touched by your story," Sarah said encouragingly. "Do you mind if I ask you a couple of questions though? Just to check in?"

"Sure! Fire away," Celeste responded.

"Okay, well first, will you tell me what the interview experience was like for you? The positive and the negative?" Sarah asked.

"Honestly, and I'm not just saying this because you're the one who interviewed me," started Celeste, "it was a really great experience. I felt heard and understood. I didn't feel like you tried to get me to say things a particular way. You just let my story exist. The only negative was that I was aware the whole time that I had a night class to get back to. I don't think I even told you that at the time, but in the back of my mind I knew I needed to make sure we wrapped up at a certain time. That was hard for me."

"That makes sense," said Sarah. She made a mental note to check in with future storytellers about hard cutoff times. "Is there anything you wish you would have said differently?"

"Maybe a little when I was talking about my dad and stepmother. I've been thinking about that some. A lot of the community knows who they are, and I know most people are aware they weren't great parents, but it's hard to say it explicitly. I still love them, and I don't want to publicly shame them. I was just being honest with everything in the moment and not as focused on who might be hurt by what I was saying," Celeste said slowly.

"I think we can take measures to make sure that what we include, if anything about that time, still honors them. I actually think that's an important note," Sarah said.

Celeste smiled and said, "Thank you! I truly could not feel more taken care of. I'm proud of who I've become, and I want other kids to know that they can go through hard things and still go on to do great things."

Sarah ended the call by thanking Celeste again and asking if she would reach out if she needed any additional support. Celeste promised that she would.

Sarah packed up her bags and headed home for the night. She was so excited to start editing Celeste's story in a couple of days!

Application: Wrapping the Interview

As you just got to experience with Sarah and Celeste, there are two endings to every interview. The first ending happens when you literally can't think of another thing to ask that would benefit the story. I call this the Soft Stop.

During the Soft Stop, ask the storyteller if you can take a short break. Offer them a beverage and let them know you are going to spend a few minutes working through your list of questions to ensure you have covered everything.

The StoryFind Soft Stop Checklist is the perfect tool to ensure you have what you need from an interview. Like you saw with Celeste's interview, the list looks like this:

- Do we have all of the pieces of a Story Arc?

- Do we have each piece of the Story Flow?

- Is there anything we might want to know a little more about?

- Did the storyteller emote? If no, is there still an opportunity to capture emotion?

- Are there any places we need pickup lines?

- Are there any places where we need the storyteller to answer more concisely?

- Did they speak with clarity on how our organization helped?

- Did they answer the question "What did this mean to you?"

This checklist is your safeguard against realizing with disappointment that you missed something days later when it is too late to ask. Push through that mile twenty marathon fatigue we talked about earlier, and take time to work through this list with intentionality. You will likely catch one or two things that will be incredibly important in shaping your edit.

After the Soft Stop, sit back down with your storyteller and fill in all the gaps. This typically takes an additional ten to fifteen minutes, and it serves to tie up the loose ends so you won't have to worry about them later. That brings you to the second ending, the actual end to the interview. At this point, you can thank your storyteller, triple check that there is nothing else they would like to add, and then walk them through logistics of what they can expect to happen next.

Aftercare

The process of aftercare depends on the storyteller and type of story you told. You can be intuitive with it—this section isn't prescriptive. We talked about revictimization earlier, but one thing that is especially important is doing follow-up with your storytellers whose stories contained past trauma. It is common for those with anxiety to ruminate on what they said or didn't say, how they said something, etc. At the end of an interview, it is important to let your storyteller know that they are still in charge of what will be shared with the world.

Just as Sarah did in our KidsKan example, we recommend having a phone meeting with your storyteller about a week after the interview. Start by letting them know that nerves after the fact are normal, and let them know that they will have the opportunity to weigh in before the story is shared.

We are often editing our stories right away, so that first phone call usually hits in the midst of our first round of edits. At StoryFind, we typically do three rounds of revisions and bring a storyteller into the process after the second round. We have only rarely had anyone ask to change content, which is actually pretty cool to think back on! If you take great care of your storytellers, you are miles ahead in finding the pieces of their story that display them in the most favorable light.

We also recommend doing a follow-up with your storyteller after their story is shared. They may feel a little jarred from the experience, especially if their story is being shown at a live event to a large audience. Their vulnerability is very much on display, which can sometimes create mental health challenges. Because of this, I recommend a debrief with every storyteller after their story is shared. You can put together a handful of questions to help assess how they are feeling:

- How do you feel after seeing your story shared at the event last week?
- What was the experience like for you?
- Is there anything you wish had been different?
- We are so thankful you shared your heart. Will you let us know if you need any additional support going forward?

This check-in is all most people need to put their fears to rest after sharing their story. However, if someone is experiencing persistent intrusive thoughts about the experience, please connect them to support with a licensed professional counselor or psychologist.

Conclusion: Wrapping the Interview

As you have seen throughout the book, my goal is to help you take amazing care of your storytellers and also accomplish your goals. Wrapping an interview well ensures you accomplish both. Let me be your cheerleader now: I know you're going to finish asking your interview questions, and all that is within you will want to be done at that moment. But please push on! Unless you're like me in the middle of New York City about to pass out in the heat as the relentless noise of bulldozers echoes in the background, I know you can make it to the end. Do a Soft Stop. Review your checklist. Do your due diligence of filling in any gaps in your story and messaging. Your more rested self will thank you later.

Reviewing what we learned here: remember to conduct a Soft Stop and review your checklist before the interview officially ends. In the days after the interview, make sure to follow up with your storyteller at least once. Allow them to weigh in on the edit once you feel it is in a good place. And finally, make sure to check in with them one last time after their story is shared.

CHAPTER 8

FINDING THE EDIT

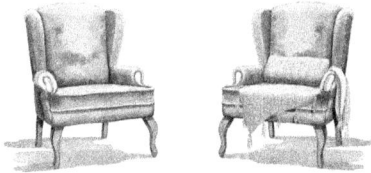

When you take it piece by piece,
you are much less overwhelmed
and much more focused on
what can stay and go.

E DITING PUTS ALL THE PIECES together and is the fifth and final step in the StoryFind Process. There isn't a right or wrong way to edit, so long as you're working toward cutting content to shape your vision as it aligns with your Master Plan. Sometimes during an interview, new information surfaces that takes your story down a slightly different path, but most often, you are editing to the Story Arc or Story Flow that you put in place ahead of time. As long as you're working in that direction, you're doing just fine!

Before we dive into how-tos, I want to remind you of the most important thing in the editing process: anchoring yourself. Do this by immersing yourself in your Master Plan. Review your Story Arc or Story Flow and remind yourself why and how you are telling your story. Adrenaline and excitement can take over if you hear a good rabbit trail during an interview, and sometimes those stories are so tempting to follow. Most often, they are not the story that will accomplish your goals. When you begin to edit, ground yourself with what you know will work.

This chapter outlines an editing process rather than specific editing tools. No matter your skill level, this gives you a road map for achieving a great final cut. Once you have a few stories under your belt, my guess is you'll start developing your own processes. Until then, I want to invite you into this step-by-step approach for crafting an amazing edit. Sarah is about to learn it all, so let's walk through it with her and then I will take you through each phase.

The KidsKan Story: Finding the Edit

Editing day dawned, and Sarah wasn't sure what to expect. The StoryFind editing process was broken up into several phases designed to make it attainable even for someone like her, with very little experience.

Like everything else in the StoryFind Process, she decided to take it one step at a time and not look ahead until the phase she was working on was complete. Sarah wanted to feel as relaxed and focused as possible, so with her laptop in tow, she headed to her favorite local coffee shop and settled into a corner booth.

Sarah's Master Plan and Story Flow

Officially, step one of her work for the day would be to review her Master Plan and Story Flow. There in front of her were reminders of her goals, how she would define success, her target audience, and her One Big Idea. She read them quietly:

Objective: To raise funds to build two new playgrounds

Define Success: Raising $150k

Target Audience: People who:

- Care deeply about systemic change in our community and believe that creating that change starts in childhood
- Are concerned about the safety and development of our community's children
- Are motivated by seeing real change and feeling like they are making a difference

One Big Idea: Playgrounds are key to creating healthy children.

She also reviewed her logistics section, which read:

Story Medium: Video

Target Length: Three to four minutes

Call to Action: To be determined

Placement: Fall gala, newsletter campaign, social media

Reviewing this information first meant that Sarah was oriented in the right direction before making any content decisions. Everything she would keep or dismiss would be in line with her project's goals.

Once she was satisfied that her Master Plan was basically memorized, Sarah pulled up her Story Flow and reviewed it all. Her initial Story Flow read like this:

- Early Childhood
- Foster Home
- Time at KidsKan
  1 First KidsKan Experience
  2 The Playground Being Built
  3 The People Who Inspired Her
- Reunification with Mother
- Current Life
- Law School
- Overall Impact of KidsKan on Celeste's Life/Where She Would Be without Us
- Hopes for the Future of Our Community
- The Ongoing Need for KidsKan

She made a mental note of her commitment to honor Celeste's desire not to focus too much on her father and stepmother. She also remembered that they had decided not to talk about Celeste's reunification with her mother.

It was at this point that Sarah opened her computer. Jeff had organized a timeline for her in the basic editing software he recommended and also sent her a link to the entire interview. Sarah had listened through it a couple of times leading up to today.

Jeff created different tabs on her editing software's timeline, and each tab was labeled with one of her Story Flow headings. Under each heading, Jeff had placed any content that went along with it. He hadn't made any cuts;

he had simply organized it into sections so that Sarah could easily edit each topic on its own rather than trying to conquer the hour-long interview without any structure. Sarah noticed that he included a Miscellaneous header for content that didn't naturally fit a Story Flow header.

Sarah's First Pass

Breathing deeply, Sarah was ready to begin making her first editing pass. She reviewed StoryFind's guidelines and goals. She would work to cut each section by 50 percent, which would result in about thirty minutes of footage left after her first pass. She consoled herself with the thought that she would be able to keep a lot and that most of the hard decisions would come a little later.

StoryFind's guide said that in this pass, she should keep everything that:

- Serves her Master Plan
- Contains emotion that drives the story forward
- Could serve as a bridge or connector between sections
- Piques her own interest or curiosity

She would cut everything else. Headphones on, Sarah started with the very first section and began whittling away. There was about ten minutes' worth of content in the Early Childhood section, and with the parameters in mind, Sarah marveled at how quickly she was able to cut it down to five minutes. She followed the same pattern with each subsequent heading, and by midafternoon, she had successfully reached her goal: only thirty minutes of interview content remained on her timeline. She could have kept going, but she decided it was more important to create breathing room for herself in between editing sessions. She wanted to approach each pass with fresh eyes.

Thirty minutes was still a lot of content, so Sarah made the decision to have this draft transcribed before moving into the second editing phase tomorrow. She quickly shared the link with an online transcription service and decided to call it a day. Armed with the satisfaction that the next day she would be working with only half of the content she had started with this morning, Sarah headed home for the night.

Sarah's Second Pass

Sarah arrived back at the coffee shop early the next day. She carried a printed copy of the transcription that had arrived in her inbox that morning, and she was ready to see what the day would hold.

StoryFind called the second pass the "creative phase." This phase of the process would be less formulaic and more instinctive with the goal of cutting the content down to within five minutes of its final target length. Sarah was both excited and nervous. She was ready to listen, feel deeply, and trust her gut with what content should stay and what content should go.

Sarah decided to edit the transcript five pages at a time and then edit the video portions, alternating back and forth. At times, she found that something sounded good on paper but not as good on the video. For example, one time Celeste said, "KidsKan is truly the best thing that ever happened to me." Sarah wanted to include that line, but when she watched Celeste say it on the video, the emotion just wasn't there—even though it was a powerful statement!

Nonetheless, using the paper transcript, Sarah hopped back and forth between striking lines on a page and cutting video. She was surprised that she had only about seventeen minutes of content left at the end of her first time through the creative phase. Her own personal goal was to get it down to seven minutes by the end of the day.

It had been about four hours, and Sarah packed up her bag and decided to head into the office for a change of scenery. So far, her strongest sections were:

- Early Childhood
- Foster Home
- Time at KidsKan
- Overall Impact of KidsKan on Celeste's Life/Where She Would Be without Us
- The Ongoing Need for KidsKan

Secondary were:

- Hopes for the Future of Our Community
- Current Life/Future Life Plans/Law School

After lunch and a team meeting, Sarah had about two hours left to accomplish her goal of getting the video to about seven minutes long.

Her instinct told her that she really needed to tighten up the early childhood and foster home sections. Celeste had asked that she not go into depth on the first part, and while Celeste's time with her foster mother, Kimberly, was important, exploring it in detail was not necessary. In fact, it could really just serve as the link that brought her to KidsKan.

Sarah focused her energy on those two sections first and was able to cut about three minutes. Glancing at her Messaging Strategy, she reminded herself that her goal in telling this story was to raise money to build playgrounds. With that in mind, she really dug into Celeste's time at KidsKan to narrow its focus on her friendship with Presley and their experience with the playground.

The playground had sort of an arc of its own, and Sarah smiled as she read that section. Celeste talked about the sadness of life before the playground, the excitement of the first day they were able to experience it, and finally the significant impact the playground had on her life. For now, that section remained the strongest and the longest. She cut about two minutes of content that diverged from the playground story in order to keep the arc intact.

Similarly, Celeste's hopes for the future of their community, while powerful, did not fully align with the Master Plan or add any pertinent content. Cutting that section took another two minutes off the video.

Finally, Sarah combined Celeste's current life, future plans, and law school into a few short sentences. In the end, the video was about seven and a half minutes. Sarah was ecstatic.

The video was still segmented into sections on her timeline, so she hadn't listened through it all start to finish. She wanted to do that now, but she stopped herself as she needed to head out the door to meet her friends for dinner. She knew she would keep working on it all night if she could! Sarah wondered how the sections would connect together. Would it all make sense? Would there be gaps where the topics didn't naturally flow from one to the next? Tomorrow she would find out!

Sarah's Third Pass

First thing in the morning, Sarah slipped into her desk chair, threw on her headphones, and watched her cut from start to finish. Seven and a half minutes flew by, and she sat back wondering if that was too long or if she could get away with the length. There were a few places that needed to be smoothed out, but she felt so attached to every piece of the story that she couldn't imagine letting anything go.

She sighed a long sigh. StoryFind had talked about this. She had just read up on the third editing pass and knew that she was supposed to trust her past self and get it to the length she initially desired it to be. Cutting it to three or four minutes seemed almost impossible, though, so she decided to enlist Maria's help.

"Maria," Sarah called down the hall, too impatient to walk to her office door.

Maria poked her head out, surprised. "Everything okay?"

"I mean, in theory," Sarah said, only half kidding. "I can't cut this story down any more than it already is!"

"And you want my help?" Maria laughed.

"Yes! Please!"

"All right, give me two minutes," Maria said, ducking back into her office.

After two of the longest minutes of Sarah's life, Maria appeared at her door. "Ready?"

"Ready and nervous!" Sarah said. She realized that this would be the first time Maria saw her work, and she had no idea what she would think. "It's currently about seven minutes and thirty seconds. I'd love to get it down to three to four minutes."

"What are you looking for from me?" Maria asked.

"I'd love to know what you think overall, of course," replied Sarah, "But I also want to know what keeps your attention and what feels long. I'm at the point where I'm having a hard time letting anything go, but I know that I'm biased."

Maria nodded and grabbed a notebook to jot down any reflections she might have in the moment. For the next seven and a half minutes, Sarah bit her nails and tried to avoid staring at Maria, as she wondered what she was thinking. Did she like it? Did she think she'd made a mistake with this whole storytelling thing? This was Sarah's first attempt, but what if it would also be her last?

"Wow," Maria said slowly. "That was not what I thought it would be. You did that?"

"Yes," said Sarah tentatively.

"That is phenomenal," Maria said in all seriousness. "There isn't any music or anything other than the interview content, the cuts are still choppy"—Sarah was only editing with the wide angle—"and yet I couldn't take my eyes away. This is more than I'd hoped for."

"Really?"

"Yes! Truly. I see why you're having a hard time letting anything go. I don't know if my notes will get you any closer, but it'll at least give you some thoughts on what I loved and what was maybe good content but didn't drive anything forward." Maria passed her paper to Sarah.

"Thank you! Seriously. I am so honored to be tasked with telling our stories. This one will always hold a special place in my heart for being my very first one," Sarah said. "I appreciate your feedback, and I'll get started trying to tighten this up."

Sarah spent the rest of the day implementing Maria's feedback. She ended the day with a five-minute cut. She submitted it again to the online transcription service, still determined to achieve her target length. She couldn't see anything else to cut in the video version, so maybe seeing it in print would help.

The next morning, Sarah finished the third phase within thirty minutes using the transcription. It was a lot easier to see which sentences could be cut on paper, and when all was said and done, she arrived at her four-minute goal.

She watched through it from start to finish and then asked and answered the following questions:

- Does this story accomplish my goals? *Yes!*
- Will this story connect with my target audience? *If this doesn't, nothing will.*
- Is my One Big Idea clear? *Definitely, yes.*
- Was my target length accomplished? *Yes!*
- Is a Story Flow or Story Arc clear? *Yes.*

Sarah was extremely satisfied with her story, but there was still some work to be done. For one thing, the edit was choppy, but that is why she had requested two camera angles during production. She knew she could cut back and forth between the two. It also needed music, and Jeff and Paul had filmed some really simple B-roll of the fire truck, the empty playground lots at the new KidsKan buildings, and some portraiture of Celeste. The fourth pass would be when she made her project beautiful.

Sarah's Fourth Pass

As Sarah read through the StoryFind material, she was pleased to see that she was heading into what she thought would be lots of fun. Her goal now was to *show* the audience rather than just *tell* them Celeste's story. It was also to bring the emotion of the story to life in new ways through the power of music and beautiful imagery.

She found some music she loved with a quick web search for inexpensive stock music and laid it in right away. Everything came to life for her at that moment. Sitting alone at her desk, Sarah cried happy tears. What had seemed impossible initially was now a vibrant story, alive with emotion and power.

From there, she added in the second camera angle—cutting to the closeup shot to evoke more intimate moments and to cover any awkward edits. Finally, she went through her B-roll and added it in places she thought would be most appropriate.

Watching it through from start to finish, Sarah knew she could work on it forever, but it was well after hours and she was meeting Jeff in the morning so he could help her smooth out a few rough edges.

Sarah's Ending

The next morning, Sarah sat with Jeff at the same coffee shop where she had started her editing.

"This is really amazing, Sarah," Jeff said. He was extra impressed since he had been there with her and knew how much she had to cut to get to where it was. "I do have a question for you though. Before I work on balancing your audio and doing some basic color correction, do you want a call to action at the end?"

Sarah blushed. In all her enthusiasm, she forgot she wanted to put a simple action item at the end of the cut. At the gala, she planned on making a live ask after the video played, but she also planned on sharing the video in several different ways beyond the event. It absolutely needed a call to action. "Yes! I do," she said emphatically. "What do you think of saying 'Visit our website to fund new playgrounds and change lives'?"

"That sounds good to me," Jeff said. He added in the call to action, applied some simple color correction, and audio balancing. After Sarah looked through it one last time, she was happy to say that from her perspective, the project was complete.

She sent the edit to Celeste, who called her within fifteen minutes to tell her she loved everything about it. She expressed that her nerves were gone and she was now fully excited to share her story with the world.

Application: Finding the Edit

What do you think? Are you ready to put all the pieces of your story together? You've made it to the final step of the StoryFind Process. If you're editing a written story, the process is easier, but when working with video, you may also be learning new technology along with trying to edit your story. I want to urge you to give yourself grace. If you need help with the technical side of your edit, don't be afraid to reach out to someone—especially as you are first learning!

Just like for Sarah's project (and all of our projects at StoryFind), in most cases, you will not be publishing a full, unedited interview. Your project will likely require editing.

Through multiple passes, you will shape and reshape your story into something both beautiful and effective.

The technicalities of editing differ depending on your medium. If your story is a print interview, you use different systems to create drafts than if you are editing a video, for example. As I mentioned earlier, because of this variety, I am going to outline an editing methodology rather than recommending specific programs and systems. While those things change over time, and editing software comes and goes, a good methodology remains steadfast through it all.

Your Master Plan and Story Flow

So, let's start back at the very beginning. Editing is storytelling in its own right. And connecting people to the story you are telling outweighs any other consideration in editing (like, "We have to include this person because of x, y, and z") and should be what you focus on the most. If you did the work to organize up front, the editing process will be considerably less labor intensive.

The first step is to revisit your anchor, your Master Plan. You want to orient yourself in the right direction—making sure that everything you keep aligns with your project's goals and will connect with your target audience. You also want to make sure that your One Big Idea emerges crystal clear in the final cut; review it before you begin to edit so that it is fresh in your mind.

Your Story Arc or Story Flow serves you in a similar capacity. The beauty of the work you did early on is that you aren't starting from scratch in the editing process! Just as Sarah did, I recommend creating headings that correspond with your Story Flow headings on a timeline or in a Word document. This compartmentalization, especially in the beginning, helps you focus on the most powerful pieces for each section.

Reviewing the Master Plan and Story Arc or Story Flow ahead of time brings focus to your video and avoids creating something that wanders around and loses impact. As you remember from earlier in the book, you don't want to make stew. Reviewing your Master Plan and following your Story Flow or Story Arc in the editing process put some safety rails in place—ensuring that what you keep is useful. You can make cuts with confidence, knowing that even if the material is good, it is being eliminated because it does not serve the project well.

Listening and Organizing

Once you have reviewed your Master Plan and Story Flow, sit down and listen to your interview from start to finish. Don't do anything with it; just listen. You'll notice places where you are rapt with interest and times when your mind wanders away to other things. Simply notice these things.

After listening to it with fresh ears, it's time to begin organizing. As you reviewed your Story Flow or Story Arc, hopefully you created tabs or headers that correspond with its sections. You can now move pieces of your interview under each corresponding heading, or drag it all onto a timeline in your editor and start organizing it there. Listen through your interview again and move content under the appropriate heading as you go.

The end result should be content laid out according to your Story Flow. There will, of course, be parts of your interview that don't correlate with the initial Story Flow. If you feel that they are parts of the story you may end up keeping, go ahead and create additional headers for them. Anything else can go under a Miscellaneous header. Do not scrap any content at this point. Simply organize.

Your First Pass

After you've revisited your Master Plan and organized your interview, you are ready to begin making cuts and selects. This process can be overwhelming if you're looking at the whole interview. Most of our interviews are an hour long (on average), which is why the organizing stage is so crucial. When you take it piece by piece, you are less overwhelmed and much more focused on what can stay and go. Just as Sarah did, take your first pass section by section with the goal of ending up with about 50 percent of the content saved and 50 percent cut in each section.

This first pass is often the easiest because you get to hold onto a lot. It is also usually very clear what needs to go—like when your storyteller rabbit trails or when your attention wanders from what you are listening to.

As a general rule, keep everything that:

- Serves your Master Plan
- Contains emotion that drives the story forward
- Could serve as a bridge or connector between sections
- Piques your own interest or curiosity

Everything else can go in this first pass. Make a goal to stick with a section until 50 percent of it has been cut. In the end, if you started with a sixty-minute interview, you should end up with approximately thirty minutes of content.

Your Second Pass

It is vitally important that you let time pass between your first and second editing passes. For the purpose of this book, I am systematizing the editing process for you and giving you a framework to work from. But the reality is, storytelling through editing is creative.

Creativity demands and requires space. It is less formulaic, more instinctive, and it asks that you trust yourself in ways that may feel uncomfortable or uncertain. The beauty of the second pass is that it allows that creativity to come to life within the constraints of the Master Plan and Story Flow. You're going to have to make tough decisions, but the goal of this pass is to get your story down to within five minutes of its target length—only slightly longer than you intend the final cut to be.

Our brains operate based on two systems of decision-making. The first is instinctual, and it happens almost instantaneously. The second operates on a conscious level and is more deliberate and slower to respond. The second editing pass of your interview relies heavily on intuition, and the third pass is made with conscious, deliberate effort.

For those of you squirming at the thought of relying on your own intuition, take heart! There are ways to cultivate it, and intuition is less exotic than those who possess a lot of it would like to think. Researchers at Leeds University concluded that intuition happens as the brain uses past experiences and cues from the self and the environment to make a decision. It happens so quickly that it doesn't register on a conscious level. When it comes to storytelling, the more you do it, the more you develop intuition around what should stay and what should go. Don't be discouraged if your first stories take a little more time as you develop your storytelling chops. If you're interested in honing your intuition, the website HeySigmund.com brilliantly outlines nine ways to cultivate it.

Being a successful storyteller requires cultivation of instinct. It takes vulnerability and honesty. It means listening without judging—both to yourself and to the story you are telling. It needs space to thrive and asks that you trust your gut. Truly, this is the hardest section of the process to teach because it is not formulaic. In the second pass of your edit, nothing is right or wrong. You are operating only on your ability to trust your instinct, attune to the pieces of the story that speak to you, and make cuts as your heart guides you.

As you work through each section of your Story Flow, you may find a section or two that you want to scrap entirely. That's okay too! Keep the essentials and the pieces of the story you've grown to love. Lose anything that isn't vital. Stick with the heart of the story. You're going to do great!

Your Third Pass

As with your first and second pass, take some time before editing your third pass. When you start the third pass, your story should be no more than five minutes longer than your target length. Up until this pass, I recommend editing in sections based on the headers of your Story Flow. But now it is time to merge everything together. Then watch it all the way through. Make notes on what makes sense or doesn't. Go back and look for lines that could bridge any story gaps and add them in.

After this is done, you should have what feels like a complete, emotionally compelling story. The only problem is that it is too long. Everything in you will likely try to justify keeping the extra length because you are attached to the whole story. But just as Sarah did, trust your past self and get it to the length that you originally wanted it to be. Where pass two was intuitive, this phase takes conscious and deliberate editing. You will make some painstaking cuts, but the final product will be better for it.

If you have the luxury, outside opinions are incredibly helpful in this phase. Others won't share your emotional connection to the story and can be more objective in telling you which parts are working and which are not. This is also a great time to show your edits to your storyteller, as they may have opinions on what should stay and what should go.

After outside opinions are gathered, work your way through from start to finish two to three times, cutting as much as possible each time. When your final pass is complete, pull out your Master Plan once more and ask yourself the following questions:

- Does this story accomplish my goals?
- Will this story connect with my target audience?
- Is my One Big Idea clear?
- Was my target length accomplished?
- Is a Story Flow or Story Arc clear?

If the answer to any of these is no, keep working at the edit until you can say yes.

Your Fourth Pass

Until this point, you have been working with content only. If your story is in print, you're close to being done; however, hold on because there is one final step, which we will reach at the end of this section.

If you are telling a story through video, once your content is locked, your final step is to add supplementary footage (video B-roll, stock footage, photography, etc.) and music. For purposes of this book, we are looking only at high-level principles behind adding B-roll and music. There are plenty of amazing tutorials out there that teach the practicalities of it all, and depending on which software you use, the process may look different. So, for now, let's just look at what is important when it comes to B-roll and music.

The goal of supplementary footage is to *show* the audience what the storyteller is talking about. It also serves a practical purpose: it covers any rough edits. All supplemental footage should serve to enhance the audience's experience of the story. If at any point the audience is thinking more about what they are seeing than the story they are hearing, that creates potential problems. Focus on capturing and using B-roll that is motivated by the story and doesn't distract the audience from the overall flow.

Working with music is similar. Music sets the mood and the tone for what you would like the audience to feel. There is great emotion already in your interview content, but adding music will really take it to the next level. Your story has an arc and your music should have an arc as well. StoryFind editors look for tracks that complement the parts of the story they are trying to tell. The music shouldn't be happy if we are showing the challenge, and of course, it shouldn't be sad when we bring hope in the end.

Even though this seems obvious, it's easy to find a piece of music to slap underneath an entire video, but I want to encourage you to think through the music with the same intentionality that you have used in the process so far. You may end up needing more than one track to really tell your story well.

Try placing your music and your B-roll together. Allow yourself to edit to the beat. Let your music give you ideas about pacing, and take your time finding the perfect piece if one track isn't working.

When we see a powerful story, we can't help but be moved. The right supplementary footage and music are keys to making that happen.

To find free music resources, search "free stock music for video" in your browser. If you are editing regularly, we recommend finding a subscription service that offers a variety of high-quality music options.

Once everything is in place, it's time to polish your Porsche. Smooth out all of your transitions and rough edges. Check for grammar and spelling errors. Make sure there aren't any glitches. Correct your color, balance your audio, etc. Finally, add any names and titles to identify people on screen, as needed.

Your Ending

One final piece of advice on editing. You want to take your audience on a journey to a practical conclusion with one clear action item. Audiences give to what they understand as the need. They also require clear direction on what they can do to be part of the solution.

Your stories should all conclude with a clear call to action. This could be text on an end screen if your story is told through video, or through the words of one of your storytellers, but make sure your audience is crystal clear on what they can do in the moment with what they just experienced. The more time that elapses between their hearing the story and their ability to respond, the less likely they are to act.

Conclusion: Finding the Edit

Editing is legitimately hard work. There are people who dedicate their entire careers to the art of storytelling solely in the editing phase. Just like the rest of the StoryFind Process, the key is to take it step by step, and recognize when you might need a partner to help with some of the more technical aspects.

Take your time, remind yourself why you are telling the story, and keep it as tight as possible without losing emotional impact.

I want to give you a checklist, so you have a road map to guide you through the entirety of the editing process:

- Review your Master Plan and Story Arc or Story Flow
- Organize your interview under Story Arc or Story Flow headings
- First pass: cut 50 percent of your content
- Second pass: use intuition to cut your story to within five minutes of its target length

- Third pass: lock your cut at its original target length
- Fourth pass: add music and B-roll and polish your final product
- Call to action: finish by galvanizing your audience's response with clear direction

And that is editing in a nutshell. I recommend giving yourself substantial time to edit your first project (two to four weeks for a video; two weeks for a print piece). Your pace will pick up as you start to form your own philosophies and workflows and as you become familiar with your editing tools.

As we reach the finish line in the StoryFind Process, I would love to share Celeste's story with you in final form. It is waiting for you in the next chapter.

CHAPTER 9

THE END

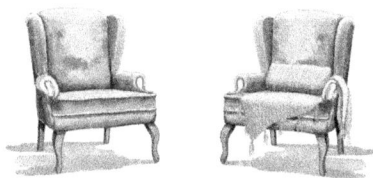

The StoryFind Process
gives you everything you need to
find and tell amazing stories.

The KidsKan Story: The End

Here is Celeste's story that Sarah shared as a video at Kids-Kan's fall gala:

Before I entered the foster care system, I lived with my father and stepmother. They weren't around much. My grandmother lived with us until she passed away when I was four. She was everything to me. When she passed away, I lost my entire sense of safety.

I know that it isn't the case for everyone, but the best thing that could have happened to me was being placed with my foster mom, Kimberly.

It was actually Kimberly who brought me to KidsKan for the first time. I was at the end of first grade, and we first came to see if the summer program would be a good fit for me. KidsKan had just moved into this building.

My whole life had been about survival. My first day at KidsKan, I actually met my best friend, Presley. I didn't feel out of place for the first time. I had a friend and a community around me that loved and cared for me.

The summer I started at KidsKan, this place was pretty empty. We had our classroom and gym, but we were basically sitting on a dirt lot. It was hard as little kids to feel like we were cooped up inside all day.

I actually vividly remember the first day we got to play on the playground—or the fire truck, as everyone called it, because it, duh, was made to look like a fire truck!

It was extremely hot the first day we got to play on it.

We all ran for the door, and there it was in front of us. It was real. It was ours! I remember playing for hours with Presley on that fire truck. Actually, years. We grew up with it. We were the first to experience the joy that came from it.

I've actually been saving my own money to give toward the two new playgrounds. I don't have much, but I know how transformative it was for me to have a safe place to play. The playground played a major role in bringing my spirit back to life.

I don't like to talk about myself, but I was admitted to law school and will be starting next year. My dreams? I want to come back here and work in foster care and adoption. Maybe one day I'll run for office. I still struggle, but if my story can change a life, then it's all worth it.

My time at KidsKan meant safety. It meant friendship. Ultimately, what KidsKan gave me was the ability to play and actually be a little girl.

Giving money to build a playground is not about play equipment. That playground meant that someone cared about us. They believed in us and wanted us to be our best.

I am who I am today because of the people who poured into me at KidsKan, the friendships that I formed here, and the people who cared enough to give their time and money so that I would have a fighting chance to do something productive in my life.

When I look back at myself as a little girl, I just want to wrap her up tight and tell her that nothing happening around her is her fault. She is not bad and not deserving of the way her parents treated her.

There are absolutely still kids in our community who are just like me that desperately need what KidsKan has to offer. They need the programs, they need the people, and they need the playgrounds. I am proof that a playground is one aspect of making a pivotal difference in a child's life.

Three months later, Sarah had raised all of the playground money for KidsKan. Two-thirds of the funds were brought in at their gala, and the other third came through the circulation of Celeste's story on social media and the KidsKan email newsletter.

Sarah was deep into her second video project—she couldn't forget Carol's request for help with the Thanksgiving dinner boxes! She had also completed three written stories, two springing from her initial pre-interviews. She was loving her work again, and the results were showing in the morale of her teammates (who needed to hear the stories as much as anyone) and in donor dollars, which were up substantially.

Even though it had been a few months, she checked in one last time with Celeste, who was amazed that her story had had such an impact. Similarly, the StoryFind Process had made a lasting impact on Sarah's life. She not only had her dream job telling stories for her favorite organization, but she also had a framework to tell the stories effectively. Life was good. Sitting at her desk reflecting on how she had been ready to quit only a few months earlier, Sarah smiled. She felt she had been given a great gift in the StoryFind Process, and one she would not soon forget.

Application: The End

You did it! I'm so proud of you. I hope as you have reached the end of the book, you have told one story that you are truly happy with. And if you haven't started the process yet, you are now fully equipped to tell any story that comes your way.

Of course, not every story fits perfectly into the Story-Find Process, but I hope it gives you a proven framework to begin telling your stories with purpose, so you can drive outcomes and results for the organization you love so much.

A lot has changed in the world of nonprofit storytelling. It used to be that we shared so much of the need but not enough hope (think DRTV in the '90s). Then the pendulum swung to the other side, and we all said we needed to see more hope and less need (which communicated that donor support wasn't necessary). I think we finally are at a place where the balance of the two is appreciated. We are able to see that stories need it all: challenge, struggle, and resolution.

And listen, not every story will be a home run. There are always going to be outside factors that influence whether or not your best laid plans turn into your best results. Maybe Kenny Chesney will helicopter in to do a sound check during your interview. Or the building next door will be in demolition. Maybe tornado sirens will go off, or ten members of your team will insist you wear headphones so they can feed you interview questions in real time. Maybe the Washington Wizards will start warming up for their game as you film in the stands. Maybe an interviewee will get cold feet or tell you they lied during their Discovery Interview. Maybe someone will add something to their story on interview day that transforms the direction of the piece entirely. All of these things have happened to me. But the thing is, when there is a solid plan in place and you know what you need from a story, it actually gives you the freedom to adapt. In every one of those situations, we still walked away with wonderful stories despite the outside influences.

My wish for you is that you will find the same to be true: that the StoryFind Process gives you everything you need to find and tell amazing stories. I want to take a moment to review before we say goodbye. Here is the StoryFind Process one more time:

- Create a Master Plan
- Find and Select Your Best Stories
- Organize Your Stories
- Interview with Skill
- Edit for Maximum Impact

You discovered how to create a Master Plan—your organizational anchor for ensuring that your stories are told with purpose. When you tell your stories with purpose, your audience sees through the noise and engages with your organization like never before.

After you created your Master Plan, you are now equipped to find and select your best stories. You know how to conduct Discovery Interviews and have proven criteria for choosing the right (best!) story to tell.

Once you selected your story, you now know how to organize it by creating a simple Story Arc or Story Flow and then identifying emotional touchpoints and drafting interview questions.

You've also learned interview skills that allow you to go deeper and create meaningful connections with all of your storytellers. Your ability to ask questions in the right way and with nuanced techniques allows your storytellers to feel loved and cared for and gives you better interview content.

Finally, you know how to edit your stories to create focus and clarity for your audience. You know what drives an audience member from insight into a problem to acting upon what they have just experienced.

This process equips you to tell stories more effectively, so each one hits its mark. You will create deep engagement with your audience, and that means you can keep doing the work you know is making a significant impact on the world.

Which, by the way, thank you. Thank you for digging into the hard. Thank you for giving people a reason to share their stories and for giving the rest of us a reason to experience them, give to your cause, and make the world a better place.

Before you go, I want to invite you to my community: StoryFind.com. Please come meet me and my team there, get all of the resources I've mentioned in the book, and show us how you are changing the world one story at a time.

It has been my honor to walk through this journey with you, and I hope our paths cross one day soon! Until then, happy StoryFinding!

ACKNOWLEDGMENTS

WHERE DO I BEGIN? This book has required the sacrifice of so many, and I am so thankful that each one of you believed in me and the project enough to help see it through.

First, to my husband and StoryFind partner, Mike, for always pushing me to step past my fears and do the hard things anyway. Thank you for giving me the time and space to create, for offering hours of thoughtful input, and for helping me stand on my own two feet. I am thankful for your visionary spirit and your constant humility. You are one in a million.

To my daughter, Izzy, thank you for opening up new places in my heart. I hope to show you that you can do anything you put your mind to. You are my beautiful, lively inspiration, and I am so thankful for the very essence of your being.

To my parents, three sisters, three brothers-in-law, three nephews, and (almost!) niece, thank you for your love and support and future promotion of this book—ha ha!

Team StoryFind: what a gift you all are. Thank you to our directors, Karl Birchley and Bill Griepenstroh. You are fiercely talented, and your commitment to growth and the art of storytelling are second to none. Thank you for always pushing and never settling.

To our producers, Jared Staab, Ellen Kohl, and Avery Clark—what an amazing team. No one knows how much you lay down to ensure that every single person who crosses our paths is uniquely taken care of. You three are gifts that I will never take for granted.

And, of course, editors extraordinaire, Mickey Seiler and Jamie Pent. You breathe life into everything you touch and are some of the most talented, humble, and patient individuals I know.

And Alex Marsh, our admin who keeps us all in line and the business moving forward: your heart and humor bring life and light to our office. Thank you for all you do! Finally, Jacob Muff, current equipment and media manager, but who knows a year from now, because you just keep growing. Thank you for your genuine heart and caring soul. I can't wait to see what you do.

Collectively, you have all helped build the StoryFind Process. And to all of our StoryFind team from the past and in the future, I'm thankful for you too! Thank you for letting me share what we do with the world! GTS!

To my lovely team at Page Two Books, I absolutely cannot imagine doing this project with anyone else. You listen so well and have understood the heart of what I hoped to accomplish from the very beginning. Working with your team has been like working side by side with an incredibly intelligent, creative, and understanding best friend. You are the absolute dream team. In particular, to my editor, Emily Schultz, you have believed in me, championed me, and pushed this project to be more and do more. Everything you have suggested has made this project better, and you, my friend, are the reason I am so proud of the end result.

I also want to give a special shoutout to my friends at the Nonprofit Storytelling Conference, Chris and Stephanie Davenport. Thank you for creating a wonderful experience for nonprofits to learn and grow. And thank you for teaching me so much and loving my family like your own. There is no one as generous as you. (Thank you to Shanon, Josh, and Gretchen, too!)

Finally, to my readers and StoryFinders, thank you for all the work that you do in this world. I know it is usually at your own expense and often without thanks. My hope for you is that finding and telling your stories will breathe some life back into your weary souls. You are one of a kind, and I mean it when I say I hope to meet you one day. Thanks again for all you do. May this book serve to ease some of the load you bear. Love to you all, and happy StoryFinding.

SOURCES

Chapter 2

Reiss, Steven. *Who Am I? The 16 Basic Desires That Motivate Our Behavior and Define Our Personality.* New York City: Tarcher, 2000.

Chapter 3

"Trust." *Merriam-Webster.com Dictionary*, Merriam-Webster, merriam-webster.com/dictionary/trust.

"Vulnerable." *Merriam-Webster.com Dictionary*, Merriam-Webster, merriam-webster.com/dictionary/vulnerable.

Chapter 4

Guber, Peter. *Tell to Win: Connect, Persuade, and Triumph with the Hidden Power of Story.* New York City: Random House, 2011.

MasterClass. "4 Types of Narrative Writing." September 8, 2021. masterclass.com/articles/types-of-narrative-writing.

Chapter 5

"Empathy." *Merriam-Webster.com Dictionary*, Merriam-Webster, merriam-webster.com/dictionary/empathy.

Chapter 6

GoodTherapy. "Nonverbal Communication." July 2, 2021.
goodtherapy.org/blog/psychpedia/nonverbal-communication.

Mehrabian, Albert. *Nonverbal Communication.* New York City:
Transaction Publishers, 1972.

Schultz, Joshua. "How to Use Silence in Therapy and Counseling."
April 8, 2021. positivepsychology.com/silence-in-therapy.

Perls, Frederick. *Gestalt Approach and Eyewitness to Therapy.* New
York City: Bantam Books, 1981.

Chapter 8

Young, Karen. "9 Ways to Tap Into Your Intuition (And Why You'll
Want To)." heysigmund.com/9-ways-to-tap-into-your-intuition
-and-why-youll-want-to.

ABOUT THE AUTHOR

KRISTIN SUKRAW is a professional story-teller, executive producer at StoryFind Films, licensed mental health practi-tioner, and national speaker. She has worked with large international non-profits, small shops, and everything in between to bring their stories to life and help them accomplish their fundraising goals.

Kristin began her career as a mental health counselor but soon found herself immersed in the world of film production for nonprofits. Through her work at Story-Find Films, she has worked with hundreds of individuals to give voice to their stories, all while helping nonprofit organizations raise millions of dollars through storytelling. Kristin's greatest passion is helping people find their voice and sharing their stories with the world.

When not on the road interviewing or speaking, Kris-tin lives in the great state of Nebraska with her husband and business partner, Mike, daughter, Izzy, and black fluffy cat, Lily.

TELL STORIES.
CHANGE THE WORLD.

Are you ready to start finding and telling your most impactful stories?

Visit **storyfind.com** for all the resources you'll need to start your StoryFind journey.

To book Kristin for speaking or training, visit:
kristinsukraw.com

For film production inquiries, visit:
storyfind.com

Connect with Kristin on Instagram:
@kristinsukraw
@storyfindbook

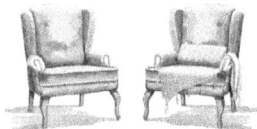

www.ingramcontent.com/pod-product-compliance
Lightning Source LLC
Chambersburg PA
CBHW030503210326
41597CB00013B/769